THE COGNITIVE SWITCH®

TURN OFF SELF-SABOTAGE AND TURN ON SELF-EMPOWERMENT, LIKE A FLICK OF A SWITCH!

SAM EVANS

authors
AND CO.

THE COGNITIVE SWITCH®

∞

I see a familiar pattern with the women I work with. Every time a client would invest in one of my coaching packages, with a desire for something BIG, they would achieve so much success, wealth and love in their lives, it's as if, like a flick of a switch, everything just fell into place.

I call this the quantum speed effect. It's so fast, you don't see it coming.

IT JUST HAPPENS.

According to Google, **switch** is defined as *'an act of changing to, or adopting one thing in place of another,' whereas* **cognition**, *is defined as 'the mental action or process of acquiring knowledge and understanding through thought, experience, and senses.'*

By reprogramming your current conditioning, you have to become the person ready to reach that next level by flicking that inner switch from self-sabotage to self-empowerment to achieve more of what you want, to BE MORE of who you want,

WITH THE BELIEF THAT YOU CAN HAVE, BE AND DO *WHATEVER YOU WANT.*

With openness, gratitude, and appreciation of where you came from and who you are, by reprogramming your subconscious mind, you are no longer controlled by your past conditioning and instead, YOU have a deep knowingness that everything will always work out because you trust you.

This is my book for you to help you turn on your self-empowerment like *a flick of a switch*, because you deserve an abundant life full of love, joy and happiness when you take back your power, simply by starting from within.

∞

WELCOME TO THE COGNITIVE SWITCH®

I dedicate this book to every single one of you who has allowed me, trusted me and chose me as your guide. If it wasn't for you, then I wouldn't be here and for that, I am forever grateful. Thank you for coming into my life and making this possible.

Most importantly, I dedicate this book to my one true love, my other half, my gift from God, my husband Barry, for this journey of evolution, would never have ever happened, without you by my side.

To my boys, Micah and Joshua, the ones who nicknamed me the Mind Doctor; for being my inspiration and supporting me, whilst mummy makes an impact.

And not forgetting, Authors & Co; for helping me put my knowledge, wisdom and power into this book. I don't know what I would do without you.

THANK YOU.

I LOVE YOU.

(AKA the mindset queen, aka B, aka Mummy)

~x~

CONTENTS

Part IV
INTEGRATION

INTRODUCTION

∞

The only way to achieve unlimited success is when YOU believe you can!

INTRODUCTION

Hello you!

∞

First and foremost, I want to say a massive thank you to you, the gorgeous woman that you are, because you not only decided to make a change in your life, but you are here, reading this book.

Initially, I wanted to begin writing this book with "*Oh my god! I can't believe I am writing this book!*" In fact, I did do that in my book collaboration I wrote in 2020 however in this case, that would be a lie. Of course, I am writing this book! It has been a dream of mine so why deny it!

We as humans tend to not acknowledge the power that we are, and brush compliments away as if we cannot believe it's possible. Anything is possible when you put your mind to it – you simply **have to believe**.

I didn't have a clue what path I was going to embark on until one day at the prime age of seven years old, I prayed hard for God to take me back, as I was sick and tired of my life. I was fed up with being shouted at, beaten, and abused. Surrounded by so much negativity, I had enough and I just wanted to quit life.

Every day I would get down on my knees, and pray:

"Dear God, please take me back. I don't want to be here anymore."

I would literally squeeze my hands, and cry until one day, I received this message:

"No. You were born for something more."

It was at this point I realised that something special was waiting for me, I just had no idea what it was.

I look back now and strongly believe that anything we go through, we grow through to help not only ourselves but also others as well. That we, spiritually live in a human vehicle, *our vessel*, that allows us to flow in life with ease. But as a seven-year-old, how on Earth was I to know about my spiritual connection to God?

This is why I am going to share everything I have learned and experienced with you in this book, because believe you me, you are not alone. You are not the only one who thinks that you are not good enough, (*believe me, you truly are*). You just have to understand where the problem started and begin the rewiring process so you can have, be and do, whatever it is you want by reprogramming your subconscious mind.

So why are you here?

Why have you now purchased another book to add to your collection of self-help books?

You are here because you are searching for something.

You feel like something is missing, as if there is a piece of the jigsaw puzzle in your brain that you cannot seem to locate - **the switch to fulfilment, empowerment and completion**. No matter how much you try, work hard and invest, you feel as if you are on a hamster wheel of chaos and overwhelm, going around and around the vicious cycle, causing you to burn out and are left feeling fed up that nothing has changed.

 "When you change the way you look at things, the things you look at change"

— WAYNE DYER.

We, as women, have been conditioned in the past century that we are excellent multi-taskers, that we can work well under pressure and that we can work hard at anything we do - **alone**.

How's that working out for you?

I can tell you now, this was the exact message that I had on my CV when I used to work in the city as an executive assistant for some of the largest investment banks in the world.

I used to believe and state that '*I worked well under chaos and pressure.*' As much as it sounded good on paper, this systematic way of thinking, feeling and behaving, actually caused complete chaos in my life. My desk would be so disorganised and flooded with papers, that by working under pressure just put more pressure on me. I would constantly take breaks just to get out of the office and would smoke my little lungs out. What seemed like a good idea, was, in fact, not.

But why do we do that? Why do we put so much pressure on ourselves?

We, as women, partners and lovers, as wives, mothers and parents, CEO's and business owners, (*everything including a broom shoved up our asses*), feel that we can do anything we put our mind to (*which is true*), but are afraid of asking for help (*fear of failing and rejection*), because deep down, we worry what other people will think of us (*fear of other people's opinions*), and therefore we just get on with it. It's as if we have this genetic code imprinted in our minds and bodies that women can do everything alone and never need help.

When it comes to running a business however, especially working for yourself, you crave that success that you see everyone posting about on social media. But because of the negative voices in your head (*that inner critic that seems to tell you it's not possible*) controlling your everyday actions, you're constantly left wondering **if it's ever going to work.**

This process, using my most favourite analogy, is like jumping off Cape Greco! Which I did do, hesitantly, in Cyprus, 2000. Everyone was jumping off this high cliff, and me, not being the greatest swimmer in the world as I looked like a flappy muppet, thought, *WHY NOT*!

If they can, why can't I?

I walked all the way back as far as I could go, ran to the edge and stopped!

I must have repeated this about seven or eight times and eventually I stood at the edge, and thought, FUCK IT, and walked off the cliff.

I didn't plan it. I didn't prepare for it. I didn't do it well.

Thank the lord I didn't break my back that day because I landed ass first!

So here I was in the deep sea of Cyprus, not able to swim or tread water and I just panicked, until my sister came to save me and dragged me out of the sea.

Looking back, although it sounds quite funny, the victim mentality was taking over me as I was seeking someone else to make me feel better. Everyone was laughing at me, and I felt like a right prat!

Now let's look at you.

Can you resonate with this story? Are you someone who TRIES to make an impact? You literally get so close to making that shift, but something pulls you back? Perhaps you do take the jump and make major mistakes, and then hurry back to the surface, wallowing in your self-pity, as if everyone is judging you for the decision that you made? Instead of celebrating your jump, you feel like a complete failure because you didn't achieve the results you really wanted, causing you to brush the initial emotion, feeling and thought away. You tell yourself that *everything is fine*, yet deep down you have made an innate decision to NEVER DO IT AGAIN.

I want you to know, it's ok.

You are not alone and I for one, most certainly would recommend that you do it supervised with a professional to ensure that you land in a safe position - *especially when you decide to jump off a cliff*. Taking that leap of faith isn't supposed to be scary – it's supposed to be joyful and happy, when in that moment, you feel completely aligned and free with your choice and decision to take action.

Throughout the lessons I have experienced in my lifetime, I realised that most of the time, we don't have any idea of what we are doing, because we cannot see our blind spots. We cannot see what the problems are, or why we feel stuck and in resistance, as we haven't learned how to face them. Instead, all we do is seek to be fixed from some source of magic pill and when it doesn't work, we doubt ourselves even more and blame the pill for not working FAST.

The answer to all of your problems, the solution to make everything ok, is within you and this is where I come in.

I'm the one who is going to guide you through this process, to help you understand what hasn't worked, why it hasn't and what you can do to resolve whatever the problem is.

Most of us THINK we know what the problem is, but in fact, it's something completely different. For example, I was working with a client who had enough of feeling stuck in her life. She wanted to build a successful business online with her fitness brand, but somehow, she decided that she just couldn't do it. She tried everything, even worked with a coach who used the tools that I use, but she couldn't eliminate the block because the root cause was not established. She deeply believed that no one could get into her tiger mindset.

When we began her one-on-one coaching, I noticed that she felt a lot of resistance to me because she wasn't sure what to expect. We began to dig deeper into the cause of her blockages and the main problem causing her pain was in fact, her lack of ability to love herself and not meeting the love of her life.

This was causing her complete discomfort, compounding her limiting belief that she could NOT be a success, as she was constantly comparing herself to her family who all had children and partners with some sort of success in their lives.

We got to work straight away and within weeks, she began dating. By applying the new tools into her life, she realised that this man was not for her. This was a huge awakening moment and discovery for this client because never in her life did she ever realise what was good enough for her.

Soon after, she went on a blind date on a TV dating show. She had no idea of the man that she would meet or what to expect. When the guy arrived, she instantly thought that this guy was not for her. However, half way through the dinner date, by having an engaging conversation with him, her energy began to change as she realised that this man was in fact **"the one."**

Now you could ask what has this got to do with her business?

Because of her lack of self-belief with her love life and most importantly, with what she really wanted, she couldn't build her business with love, joy and excitement. Her mind was filled with limiting beliefs caused by past experiences that prevented her from owning her truth to identify what was most important to her, which in this case, was to have a loving relationship.

By clearing the emotional blocks from her past, she made room and energy to meet the man of her dreams and in less than a year, her life has had a complete 360. Her missing piece to her puzzle was to have love, clarity and commitment in her life and by being able to achieve this, she has been able to apply these new found behaviours towards building her own business, *exactly like she has in her relationship.* She aligned herself and turned on her success switch and attracted her dream man.

She is now happily engaged to a man who met all of her relationship values *(what's most important to her when it comes to having a loving relationship) and* still to this day, she is over the moon living in alignment to what she actually wanted. She knows her standards and raised her level of expectations whereas before, everything only existed in her head.

Can you see how the problem itself wasn't the missing piece?

It was a lot deeper.

By establishing the **root cause** of her problem at a **subconscious level**, she was able to **heal and align** to have, be and do whatever she wanted.

This is what I do.

I shine the light on the blind spots that women cannot see themselves, to help them awaken their truths, face them and address them so that they can begin to put the missing pieces of the puzzle together and create the life that they know they want, with the belief that they can.

I would also like to add that sometimes, most women do not like seeing their own reflection. It isn't always pretty. When you spend so much time hiding behind a mask, you find it difficult to even see the truth in who you are. I have this knack of asking challenging questions that requires you to start looking deep within. *I am not here to fix you, because you are not broken;* I'm here to show you how your current perception, your model of the world, is causing you heartbreak and pain, and **it's time to let it go.**

Back in 2018, I had a situation with a client who couldn't understand why she wasn't succeeding in her online business. She felt as if she was doing all the right things, but something was missing. Within her first session, I showed her reflection and she instantly went into defence mode because emotionally she couldn't face it.

By showing this client her reflection, her anger and sadness came to the surface in full throttle. She began to mock me, in frustration and started to cry, as if she were a child being told off by a parent. It was safe to say, her inner child and memories of the past were causing her major self-sabotage.

As I observed this client, I just thought, *what has happened to this soul to think and feel like this, and how can I help her?* Most people would take this personally. However as coaches, all we want to do is help people and my role is merely to help women align and heal without telling you the solution, because the answer is within you.

By the time we completed her course of coaching, her final words were,

 "*Wow. Sam Thank you! I am so sorry for how I spoke to you, thank you for leading me to my true light*."

That was a magical moment.

Success can mean something different to each and every one of us. It could be a successful relationship, a successful business, or a successful healthy lifestyle. It could be having lots of money, or an influx of clients, but whatever the results that you desire, it's only when we become present in the moment and release the burdens weighing us down, that we can finally begin the **elimination** process. By breaking free from the mental, emotional and physical blockages holding you back, you will be able to allow **clarity** to flourish through your entire being as you become fully aware of who you truly are and knowing what you want, *without having to chase it.*

So how did I become an expert in this field?

Why is it that I seem to know what works?

Well, first and foremost, there are amazing women out there who most probably do what I do, and a lot of mindset experts that specialise in the brain; however, women come to me because they just feel drawn to me. It's as if I can see them for who they truly are, allowing them to feel safe and secure knowing that they are in the right place at the right time. By intuitively listening, I help clients release the internal blocks which are causing them significant pain and confusion so that they can finally be free to be themselves.

So, let's check in with you.

How are you currently feeling?

Do you feel as if your mind is in the right place?

I must be brutally honest here for a second. Your mind is currently controlling everything you do caused by the conditioning of your past. In fact, I tell my clients when we begin their one-on-one coaching, that their unconscious mind won't trust me straight away and will do everything to pull them back. This is the fine work of the EGO, the little voice that gives you all the excuses to NOT move forward. If this is you right now, **Congratulations**! You are triggering a new way of moving forward and your subconscious mind and ego doesn't know how to respond to this and the only thing it can do is pull you back.

BUT I KNOW THAT YOU ARE READY FOR CHANGE.

This is a clear indication that you are making the right decision to do something new and break out of the box that has been keeping you feeling stuck. You now want something different, and it makes your ego uncomfortable.

Not only do I have the life experiences that support the lessons I have been through, I also have the qualifications. I actually had no intention of becoming a coach, a mentor or even an author, because I didn't know what I really wanted, and I am so grateful that the coaching path was created for me because I really did unlock my purpose. I wouldn't be who I am today or where I am today if I hadn't of gone through the journey that I have been on and that I am still on. But then the question bodes, *would I have reached this place quicker if I paid better attention and given myself permission to just be?* Who knows! This is why most people tend to question themselves and ponder,

Will success ever come to me? And if so, WHEN?

The lack of patience, trust and faith in one's journey causes a significant number of problems in one's mind!

Will I be rich? Am I pretty? Can I really make it?

The self-judgement goes full throttle, and the envious little devil appears.

Why is she better than me and making more money than me, I'm better than her!

The deep anger and frustration of not getting your results fast or ever at all, emerge to the surface.

And here you are, investing a tonne of money on books, courses, programmes and coaches, but NOTHING HAS CHANGED and the infamous doubtful question pops into the mind: *WHY DOES THIS KEEP HAPPENING TO ME?* I used to do this too - ALL THE TIME. Which is why I am so grateful when the world of NLP, Time Line Therapy® and Hypnotherapy entered my life.

As a master coach in this field, specialising in emotional intelligence, inner child therapy, silent counselling and human design, I believe that there is a greater force out there that allows us to infinitely tap into the power that we are.

That power begins within you.

Are you ready to dive in and discover what's been keeping you stuck and start seeing your desires flourish into fruition before your very eyes?

Because believe you me, IT HAPPENS!

∞Δ∞

This book has been specifically created, planned and mapped out to allow you to unlock your potential, discover your passion and purpose, with joy in your entire being.

Using my trademarked process, The Cognitive Switch®, I will be guiding you through your very own process evolution to help you establish what is causing you a major dysfunction in your life and teach you how to overcome it.

I literally say it how it is because *what's the point in sugar coating the truth?* It's not always pretty? **But you are.** You are stunning and gorgeous, and by the time you reach the end of this book you are going to be feel empowered, confident and so *fucking awesome* because you will know how powerful you really are.

By the way, this isn't a one-time read. OH NO, MOFO! *(Not being rude, just humouring you here a bit. I do that a lot.)* It's a book that you can go back over, repeatedly.

Got a problem? Read the book.

WHY?

To unlock your solution.

It's as if I am coaching you right here, right now. Supporting you to wherever you need to go and whoever you need to be.

My promise to you is that your mind will never be the same again.

I mean why would you want that? That's why you bought this book, right? To unlock your missing piece of your puzzle and turn on self-empowerment without being mind-boggled by everything out there? To FINALLY flick that switch from off to on - RIGHT?

That's the power of the Cognitive Switch®.

I got you TILL YOU GOT YOU.

Let's go!

PREPARATION

∞

No matter how others perceive you, it's how you see yourself that matters.

Your perception is your PROJECTION.

So make it your mission to create your world, your way,
just like Batman.

IMAGINE TURNING OFF ALL THE THINGS THAT DISEMPOWER YOU SO THAT YOU CAN BECOME INFINITELY EMPOWERED AS ONE. AS YOU.

Just for a second, I want you to imagine a light switch in your house. A light that you switch on to bring light into your home. When it's off, it's dark. When it's on, there is light. A switch is all it takes to lighten a room, to bring the lightness out from the darkness to help you see things clearly.

Pretty simple to comprehend, don't you think?

This is exactly what most people desire from life.

To turn off the negativity and turn on the positivity without being consumed by the darkness. There is only one light that exists. That bright spark exists within you to help you overcome all the darkness.

Rewiring and reprogramming your mindset is crucial for emotional, physical, spiritual and energetic alignment. It's the reason why I created this book to help you flow with ease throughout each chapter. It isn't just about searching for the missing piece of the puzzle, or just discovering the reason why you feel stuck and feeling more confused; it's about,

- Understanding yourself and WHY you feel stuck.
- Understanding what's been holding you back and how.
- Knowing what you ought to do, opposed to what you should.
- Unlocking your deepest power and taking back control, empowered as YOU.

Whatever it is that you are searching for, it doesn't exist outside of you – it already exists within you. When you clear away the clutter, you discover the solution to anything and everything by connecting to your true self, **when you just believe.**

IT'S ALREADY IN YOU. BOTH THE PROBLEM *AND THE SOLUTION.*

"So why can't I access it myself?" I hear you say. **Because you're solely focusing on the end result instead of enjoying the journey.**

You spend your time focusing more on what you don't have by putting all of your energy into achieving your desired result. This causes you to travel either super-fast or super slow in your vehicle, preventing you from seeing your blind spots and therefore missing out on all of the good in your life. You then feel too scared to make big moves which prevents you from making sound decisions and instead of facing any given problem, you're actually running or hiding away from them.

IT'S ABOUT FOCUSING ON THE DRIVING FORCE - YOU.

The solution is YOU.

Therefore, I will advise a few things to make this journey one that you will never forget and to leave the old way of thinking behind, so that if you ever decide to read this book again, you'll turn on another switch! If you ever read another book, you will more than likely absorb, learn and comprehend at another level, hence why I have put this book together based on how I would run my one on one and group coaching programmes, as if I am coaching you, mentoring you, whipping your ass into the present, RIGHT NOW.

How this book works.

There are five parts to the Cognitive Switch® within which are certain steps to help you break down each area, so that you can understand wholeheartedly who you truly are, without going all into all of the mindset jargon.

Get organised.

Time is used so much as an excuse when we all have the same amount of it. I would advise you to block some time out for you to do the inner work. Think of it like a coaching session with me, where you block off an hour a week - or an hour a day - as I support you in your mind unravelling journey, so you can begin to shift and pivot into the soulfully aligned self that's best for you.

Take Action.

I have added journal prompts and supportive tasks for you to act upon throughout the book, so get yourself a journal - a special one that will mean something to you - so you can use it to support you as you read this book.

This will allow you to elaborate and execute your thoughts as you flow through your inner journey. Plus, if you ever need to reflect on your learnings, growth and expansion, you have something to refer back to - SO GO GRAB A BOOK.

Trust in you.

If you think, for one minute, I am holding the key to the missing piece, **THINK AGAIN**. To truly reconnect to your identity can only ever be discovered when you apply the methods, tasks and actionable steps into your life, as you start to become more present, and follow the journey that is written for you. Therefore, this book is **YOUR** journey of evolution, it's **YOUR** self-development process and it's **YOUR** valuable lessons that will allow you to turn on your switch.

There are also three rules that I would love for you to also know, that I always express to my clients:

Be true to yourself.

Remember, this isn't about me - it's about you. It's time to put you first and start aligning to your core desires based on your design, not anyone else's.

When you come upon a question that triggers you, you will naturally want to ignore it. Your nervous system will trigger an alarm that you are about to do something out of your comfort zone, and therefore will want to find an excuse, such as doing the cleaning, *even though you didn't want to,* OR go binge watch Netflix.

FYI, I LOVE NETFLIX there is no judgement here.

However, you could potentially feel the need to procrastinate and be activating some deep limiting beliefs that will prevent you from wanting to actually change - *AM I RIGHT?* If you feel that way, **JUST PAUSE**. Anytime we consciously get excited to do something new, the unconscious will always be the victor controlling your every move. Step away, grab some H2O, stick the kettle on, make a brew and then get back to it.

It's time for you to take back control of your navigation system and heal your ego.

Also, word to the wise, when asked how you are feeling, avoid saying, *"I'm good. I'm fine. I'm ok."* **These are not feelings**. These are just mind-numbing words that disregard your true feelings, so be truthful.

Be true to me.

I want you to read this book as if I am there with you. Imagine my voice, my lovely British accent – a cross between East and

South London - supporting you and nurturing your mind. Lies
don't help anyone, so be true!

Speak your truth and be kind to yourself too. If you miss a bit, or
don't understand something, then be real! Speak up! Own yourself because *before clarity comes confusion*, so give yourself permission
to embody this book at your own pace as your soul desires, to be
infinitely free.

Follow instructions.

I cannot even begin to tell you how many times a client will ask
me for a break during their coaching. If your mind has been
conditioned for decades to hold you back, the breakthrough
process is going to test you - A LOT. It doesn't mean it's a bad
thing. It just means that you are shifting and pivoting from what
you used to know, to what you actually want to know, aligned
as you.

∞
MEET YOUR COACH

I want you to know that there are three things you should probably also know about me.

I'm no different to you, and I mean that in every possible way.
However, right now, and why I am so good at what I do, it is
because I live by three important rules:

I don't accept bullshit.

*To do anything in life, we must be honest about everything as there is no room
for BS in your life.*

When I say this, I mean, I have a low threshold for excuses. If we,
as humans, cannot speak our truth and instead simply lie, please
do tell me, how on earth is anyone ever going to live authentically

in the victor venue without the excuses, lies and the constant need to justify our behaviours?

Excuses are what we, as humans, love to give, caused by low emotional intelligence - *the innate ability to take responsibility.* I will discuss this topic much deeper in part one. However, for now, I would love for you to give yourself permission to commit to a gentle transition from victim to victor by leaving the bullshit in the fields, *as you ain't got time for bull,* and you most certainly are NOT full of shit! You're just constipated with your inner blocks and it's now time to let it go, no matter how much it hurts. *(Gross, I know!)*

I offer a safe space to communicate.

It's time to protect your space and say bye-bye whingey whinge bottom and hellooo authenticity!

This may sound pretty strange, but if we allow room for gossiping, whinging, and moaning, then we are not taking responsibility for our actions, choices or our results.

Please do note that I used to love whinging and moaning! I thought it was the Bollywood queen in me as Indians LOVE to gossip! *(If you know, YOU KNOW!)* But moaning and giving space for people to moan to you, only brings you down. WHY ALLOW THAT? It's a clear distraction from doing what you ought to be doing and instead, you are simply following what society expects from you – FITTING IN! This behaviour does not pay your bills nor ever will *unless you're acting in the latest soaps in England. DRAMA, DRAMA, DRAMA!*

I will always be honest, no matter how harsh it sounds.

I can never tell you what is right or wrong, but I can voice my opinion, thoughts and messages based on my own experiences.

As much as I have the knowledge, the tools, the certificates, and the t-shirt, I will just say it how it is. I'm not going to act/speak like I've swallowed the Oxford Dictionary; however, I will speak exactly how I normally would, as if we are on a call.

As you read this book, or hopefully listen to it in audible, I want you to imagine that I am talking to you directly with my voice. *(In case this isn't audible, go check out my website www.samevansglobal.com to hear how I speak! You'll get the jist!)*

Hopefully you are now prepared with what to expect, who I am and how I work. It's now time for **you** to get to work!

PART I
REALISATION

What's really holding you back and why.

"The only thing that's standing in your way, is you."

What you think you know:

That someone else or something else is causing you to feel, behave and think this way.

What you don't know:

That there is no one to blame, it's just your defence mechanism preventing you from taking responsibility.

What you should know:

If you keep burying everything under that rug, one day, you will trip over and hurt yourself. It's about facing the problem in a safe way, instead of hiding from it.

IT'S TIME TO CLEAN UP.

YOU WERE MEANT TO BE HERE.

∞

WHAT IS YOUR PURPOSE?

Why am I here?

What is the purpose of life?

Is life really supposed to be this hard living in survival mode?

Are we only meant to work till we retire?

Am I meant to be stuck and in resistance all of my life?

OR IS THERE SOMETHING MORE?

So many questions are embedded in the mind that cause us to worry about a future that doesn't even exist, which in turn causes major anxiety and stress to our physical body.

I, for one, even pondered the question myself, as I wrote this book.

"Why am I writing this book? What is my purpose?"

Don't think for one minute that I never question myself. The difference is, I know how to shift into a space of clarity, without worry, fear or doubt consuming every move, decision or thought I make. This is exactly what I would LOVE for you to achieve too because self-esteem, self-confidence and self-empowerment is already there waiting for you when you simply begin to unravel the problems causing the negative impact in your life.

I truly believe I was born to make an impact, to serve and to guide women to achieve their desires because if I can, then I know that YOU can too. Some people can't stand this phrase, but it's true. I know how it feels to be held back, unable to achieve your fullest potential, and how to overcome the fears.

I became a parent. I became a wife. I healed myself and became the real me.

I had to become the person I was born to be energetically, mentally, emotionally, spiritually and financially, because I knew all along that my purpose was bigger than me.

We, as humans, experience things at a human level. This basically means we live our lives based on what we believe to be true, formed and created internally from external events we experience, which can prevent us from tapping inwards for guidance. Both negative and positive experiences create memories lodged in the unconscious part of your brain, which control your every thought, feeling and behaviour. If you are consumed with negativity and lack clarity in your purpose, this will cause you to feel as if you are stuck, because unconsciously, you are still living within the problem. When you begin your growth into self-actualisation, the penny drops, and you instantly shift your inner perception and evolve from a fixed mindset to one of expansion.

I used to feel that everything was happening to me, that everything and everyone was to blame.

It wasn't my fault! It was their fault!

The thing is, we as humans, cannot always see the real reason as to why we think, feel and act the way that we do because we lack the ability to take responsibility for most of the events in our lives. Don't get me wrong, I am not here to say that any one of us are to blame for any trauma or abuse that could have happened, but we can become responsible for how we choose to move on, simply by reconnecting to our core purpose and allowing ourselves to move forward with ease. I for one suffered decades of abuse and trauma and if I hadn't of let it go, then I wouldn't be who I am today.

Feeling like there is something wrong with you is partially true. It's a clear indication that you are misaligned to your core design and being on this planet. It's only when we truly know ourselves that we can finally begin to accept that we do exist and co-create the life that we desire, because we begin to know our purpose.

Funnily enough, it was only the other day I was speaking to my boys about my purpose and my dreams, as it all began with speaking about my dream home. I have two boys, both miniature versions of me in every possible way. *I always said that if I had twins, they would have been a split personality of me. I should have been more careful with what I asked for, because sometimes, it really feels like I am arguing with myself – TWICE!*

My children are obsessed with Minecraft, and because they know how much I desire my dream home, they asked me, *"Mummy, can we create your dream house?"*. They wanted to build it on Minecraft, and I thought, *"Why not?"* Imagination really is everything! I know it was really an excuse to play the game whilst having my attention, but my God, do they have a wonderful imagination!

Once they had completed their version on paper, they transferred their design onto the game and when I saw what they had created, at the ages of seven and nine, I was literally smitten with how creative they both are.

I was so impressed, and said, *"OMG, you two could become architects!"* It then hit me that I actually did want to be an architect and I had completely forgotten about it. My youngest asked, *"Did you do it then?"* Obviously thinking I've done a million things in my life, I replied:

"No darling. I used to have a lot of dreams, but I had no idea what I wanted to do. I wanted to be a lawyer," (but being a lawyer is so different to the courtroom drama you see on the American TV shows, so I changed my mind)*; "I wanted to be a marine biologist to live somewhere hot, but I had to be a good swimmer and I wasn't. I wanted to be an air hostess but again I had to be a good swimmer, so I thought why not be a pilot? But I needed good eyesight and I couldn't do that either."*

My youngest then replied, *"But Mummy, you found your dream job now, haven't you?"* I responded, *"Yes baby. I help women with their minds".*

HE SAID, "NO, YOU'RE MY MUM".

Isn't he just a ball of mush?! He so knows how to melt my heart and his words are just as beautiful as his spirit. You see, I always wanted to be a mum. At first, it was more because I didn't want to be like my own mum. I wanted to be different and give them all the things I didn't get as a child (*sorry Mum! I gotta say it how it is*). I wanted to be able to provide love, nurture, and fun for my own children, as I didn't really receive it from my own parents as a child. I just wanted to be loved and love someone back.

I couldn't be prouder of the way my two are, *especially when they aren't bickering or arguing over the remote, or who farted in each other's face.* **Yes.** I have those problems too and as much as I love them, I really did struggle to show them and give them the love back because I just didn't know how.

But was this my only purpose in life, to just be a mum?

I mean, there is no job description, is there, or a training manual or a prescription to block out the screams and screeches. So, I guess yes, it was part of my life's purpose because I did ask for it; but deep down I knew that there was still something missing.

We have a guide to be a coach, a guide to be a teacher, a guide to cook, even a guide to show us how to drive, but no one tells us how to be a parent and when we do become one, we have to think of others, which in turn, impacts us, because we forget about us! Now, don't get me wrong, my boys are my world; but how can I serve from an empty cup, if I don't take care of myself?

How can I show up if I don't even know who I am anymore?

I really do feel that when we have children, as mothers, we lose our identity. We reminisce so much on who we were, and how life was, that we forget to enjoy the present moment with our loved ones. We dream of the day we get married and have children and when we do, we then start to remember our past selves, where we had no strings attached. We can never be happy, right? Why is that?

SELF SABOTAGE, MY LOVE – SELF SABOTAGE!

Despite my past conditioning causing me to suffer immensely with anger issues, suffering silently in fear with a personality of someone who could have been considered bipolar, I began to project my chaotic inner world into my outer world. By becoming a parent and feeling like a lost cause, my internalised perception

7

and limitations about life projected outwards faster than I could control it and I felt like a complete waste of space.

My model of the world was my model; no one else's and it was only through my own true journey of self-discovery that I realised there is never anyone to blame for who we are or what we go through. It's up to us to understand and learn from it to be able to move forward, without the self-sabotage.

∞

THE TRUTH AND NOTHING BUT.

I read a post somewhere online that stated:

"We arrive with nothing, and leave with nothing, it's what we do in the middle that matters."

So why is it, we fuss so much in between, *aka life*, for materialistic stuff?

In the early stages of motherhood, I was massively depressed, suffered with major anxiety and post-natal depression, so the only thing I could do, and really knew how to do that resembled any part of who I once was, was to work hard to make money. I just threw myself into working harder to avoid any emotional problems.

I used to be so obsessed with buying a house, getting a car, earning a six-figure income, *but is that really more important than my family, love and joy?* Through many lessons in my life, I concluded that it really wasn't. My constant need to be in the rat race was my conditioning and it was causing major discomfort in my life, especially with my family. I wasn't appreciating anything and I had this greedy nature to want more things, because nothing in my life felt good enough, simply because I didn't feel as if I was.

If we can't be happy with what we've got, then how can we expect more?

With so much pressure from society, with an expectation of what we should have and who to be, no wonder we feel the urge to achieve so much so quickly because of what everyone else is doing.

You gotta go to school! Get a job! Become a success! Get a mortgage! Settle down! Retire! And then die?

Is that all we are supposed to do?

I had no idea that my past was well and truly beginning to project deeper and deeper into my current reality which was causing major disruptions in all areas of my life. I realised that I had to do something because all of this was happening for a reason.

∞

In December 2015, I was feeling resentful and frustrated because I just had a major argument with a friend. I was desperately seeking her friendship to be needed by someone, completely dismissing that I already had three people who *did* need me.

After this argument, I asked the most gut-wrenching question to my husband:

"Baby, why is it that things keep going wrong for me? Why do I keep falling out of friendships as if everyone is attacking me?"

I can tell you now that I was not ready to hear the truth or even want to accept the truth. My ego and victim mentality were in full throttle, ready to come back with an argument, but I felt my spirit tell me, **just listen.**

He asked me, *"Are you sure you want to hear the truth?"* I said *"YES, I DO. I know I won't like it, but I have to understand and accept the truth."* He told me,

"IT'S YOU."

I obviously cried deeply and I did everything I could not to answer back, bite back, or even react with a defensive approach, as that's all I knew how to be. I knew I had to listen to what he was telling me because deep down, I knew it was true and that he just wanted the best for me.

Can you see why it's so important to be truthful with yourself?

It was at this point I literally said to myself, *"You know what, I'm done. It's time for change,"* but despite confirming acceptance, I didn't act in alignment with my words and continued to ignore the problem. I thought to myself, *'Well if that's it - cool! I accept it –* **LET'S MOVE ON!***'*

Little did I know, I was in for a shocking wake up call.

∞

EVERYTHING HAPPENS FOR A REASON.

Before I even became a coach, my entrepreneurial journey began as the founder and creator of Montessori Home from Home - a childcare business providing baby and toddler classes using heuristic play and childminding from home using the Montessori ethos. I thought, *well if I've got kids, why not work with them?*

BIG MISTAKE THAT WAS!

I had planned to move to Canada in 2009 and start afresh. Looking back now, I was in fact running away from life as I knew it, but my credentials weren't enough to apply for a visa. I knew I had to do something more.

I had just met my gorgeous husband, working as an assistant at EDF Energy, and he said, *"Why don't you become a teacher?"* I knew state school education would take me years and I was in a rush to find something faster, so I thought, *why not.*

A colleague told me to look at Montessori education. I had no idea what it was, but little did I know that this would be my first awakening experience to the world of the mind.

The Montessori ethos focuses on the prepared environment for a child between birth to five, to help support their ability to learn at the unconscious and conscious level through observation of what the child needs, guided by the directress (in other words the teacher).

This course most certainly opened the gateway of how much my past had affected me because when we reached the module on child development, I couldn't stop crying and I had no idea why which most probably explains why it took me so long to comprehend the difference between unconscious and conscious. I really couldn't understand it at the time because I lacked in emotional intelligence, and I had my past habits of *not feeling good enough* overriding everything I did.

I passed with a merit and I was so happy that I had educated myself further and achieved something else that wasn't dictated by society - much to the dismay of some of my fellow students who actually stopped talking to me because they had failed and expected me to do the same. *Nice, hey?*

I was then offered a part time role at my local Montessori nursery, where I soon fell pregnant with my second child in 2012. There was no way I could work on minimum wage and raise two children. So, during my maternity leave I decided to invest in my career further as I knew a change was coming.

In December 2013, I met the wonderful Georgina Hood, founder of Paint Pots Montessori, in London. She literally took me under her wing and mentored me in heuristic play so I could create my own business for babies and toddlers.

Despite feeling so excited, I had no idea how to run a business and it freaked the alarm bells inside of me. But Georgina could see my light and my potential and for that I am forever grateful. She was also the very first person to introduce me to Reiki and became my Reiki Master and gifted me with this incredible healing modality in 2014 with Reiki level I followed by Reiki level II in 2016.

Reiki was something new and fascinating! Hearing how women had overcome cancer, illnesses and mental exhaustion by using this energetic method, I thought, **YES!** *Let me grab this experience and knowledge too*, should it ever come handy for my own children.

When I initially completed level I, I remember that day as if it were yesterday. I left the training feeling so calm, flowy and peaceful, that everything around me felt so different. I could feel the energy and vibration from everything, as if I had a fresh slate to start again. I thought to myself, *finally!* *I'm healed!*

We were advised to do twenty-one days of self-healing to continue the process and embody the new method. The initial twenty days were a breeze, but by the time I reached day twenty-one, I remember the kids were doing something silly and instead of being this new-found soul, this perfect mum, I completely lost my shit at them. I was screaming, roaring, crying, exploding like the biggest volcano in the world and I just couldn't believe nor control how I was reacting. Thankfully, the boys didn't take me too seriously and assumed I was playing a game as monster mummy. I couldn't stop crying as they both hugged me. I couldn't understand what had happened.

Where on earth did this come from?

How can it be here after all the work I have done on myself, WHY? WHY? WHY?

But everything happens for a reason and it was time for me to seriously face my problems, no matter how much I resisted change.

That anger was nothing new. It was very, very old and so deeply buried in my soul because I hadn't faced my past. I had so many fears, feelings of rejection, limiting beliefs in my mind caused by trauma, abuse and other significant events from my life, that instead of being able to move away from the pain, they kept compounding my major self-limiting belief of not being good enough. I had pushed the anger deep into my soul because I didn't want to remember anything. My hubby always used to tell me that I needed to talk about the past, but **I just wanted to forget it all.**

"I don't want to talk about the past! I want to forget it! ***It's done!"***

But he wouldn't stop. Not the best way to approach me as a manifestor. *That's my human design,* and the thing about this version of me was that I did not like being told what to do or to be controlled. With my past conditioning, it was even more difficult for him to communicate with me, especially when all he wanted to do was help me. I know he had my best interest at heart, as I wouldn't be here if he hadn't pushed me a little; I would still have been stuck in the past.

I just wanted an easy life and the more I asked for good and ease, the harder life felt. I began to feel even more disheartened and frustrated with everyone in it.

∞Δ∞

In February 2016, when my two boys were under the age of four, I was on the nursery run before heading off to the church hall where my classes were held. I was rushing around like a headless chicken, frantic and panicking that I was going to be late and was in the most frustrated mood ever. I was so obsessed with working and having to be on time, but I was always complaining I never had enough time and I was always late.

On route to the nursery, which wasn't too far from where I worked, I had hit some traffic on the way. The nursery was literally down the road, but instead of waiting calmly and patiently, *as I was far from calm and patient back then,* I thought **fuck this**! I quickly checked my mirrors and did a quick u-turn to take a different route. As soon as I turned the car, with my windows rolled down making sure it was all clear, I heard someone scream, **"OH SHIT!"** Before I even knew it, a cyclist came speeding out of nowhere. He hit my car door and went flying over the bonnet.

I had hit my biggest fear of all time.

Although it wasn't my fault and he took full responsibility by apologising excessively for speeding so fast, it didn't help the fact that a cyclist had just hit my car which was one of my biggest fears as a driver. My children were screaming and I was jammed in the car as his bike had locked me in. I was holding up traffic and I just felt so stuck, with no idea how to get out. I was panicking, screaming and crying because my fear was well and truly consuming my entire being and my poor babies were so upset.

HOW COULD I HAVE ALLOWED THIS TO HAPPEN?

Thank God he was ok, fit and well, but I couldn't stop crying. I was in a complete state of shock, as anyone would be however, I just carried on with my day as normal in complete disbelief that this even happened.

A few days later, I was driving home after dropping the kids to nursery again. I chose to go a different route as I refused to go back down the other road and face my fear again. I began to visualise the accident in my head and instantly felt out of control. I told myself that *"Everything would be fine! Get over it. He's ok, you are ok! Move on."*

But it didn't feel right. I literally felt this ball of fire inside of me light up like this surge of power. Unknown that it was my spirit communicating with me, I put my foot on the brakes and screamed,

"NO! I am not FINE! THIS IS NOT OK!"

Thank God that there was no one behind me because I literally did put my foot on the brake. I had just realised that there was something deeply wrong with me and I really needed help because I never wanted to experience this feeling again.

This was my awakening moment where I realised how stuck I really felt in life and that everything DOES happen for a reason. Now was the time for me to seriously pay attention to my journey of healing and growth so I could become the best version of me.

I just had no idea of how or what I had to do, but I knew I had no choice but to face the music.

SAM EVANS

∞

FACE THE MUSIC.

I really believed deep down in my soul that I was just a big fat problem, and there was no solution to help me. I had this desperate need to search for help and I was constantly seeking approval because I just wanted to be valued. My self-sabotaging thoughts and limiting beliefs were so deeply embedded in my mind and body, that I really believed I was nothing, broken and unworthy to ever achieve anything good in my life and that everything I did was a complete failure and the only way to feel accepted was to be accepted by others.

I guess with my history, you could see why I did.

I had an abusive childhood full of trauma, abuse and negativity, conditioning my very existence without me even knowing.

I spent my teenage years trying to fit in, to be a part of something, but faced rejection upon rejection from school, friends, men and even jobs, unable to make trusted decisions.

I spent my twenties intoxicated on drugs and alcohol, with a £40k debt looming over my head because the only way I could feel any sort of joy or happiness was to spend. I threw every penny I could into making myself feel better, worthy of existing, via shopping, going out and drugs. The come down was NOT pretty.

It was only when I reached my thirties that I had no choice but to become the person I was born to be, which meant facing the truth about who I really was and to change my entire perception.

The past was heavily weighing me down, but I still kept pushing harder. I just wanted success and to have something that worked out for me where I could create the same level of income that I used to make as an EA in the city. I had a passion to serve, **to just**

16

help people, but I had no idea how I was ever going to be a success, feeling the way I did.

Despite running my own business and having invested over £10k into my venture, I was not seeing the return on my investment as fast as I had hoped, so I decided it was time for a change.

In 2015, I found and watched the incredible Emma Cooper become a top leader for a network marketing company called Forever Living. She literally went from broke to six figures in six weeks and completely transformed her life, by helping other people set up their own businesses and sell aloe vera products.

I thought, *well, If she can, I BLOODY CAN!*

With my experience in banking taking care of systems and teams of over thirty bankers at a time, I thought, **OMG I could so do this** and I signed up. This was when mindset and the law of attraction officially entered my life and my mindset journey really began.

Everyone kept talking about this book called **"The Secret."** I thought everyone had gone mad and that perhaps I had signed up to a cult and I felt massively triggered. I felt triggered by other people knowing more than me, triggered at others being more successful than me and I just couldn't understand why I was not achieving success as fast as everyone else. Even though I had a Montessori diploma, *which opened my pathway to understanding the mind*, and acquiring Reiki, *which helped me understand energy and healing*, I wasn't applying any of this new found knowledge into my life because I was so obsessed with making money.

Massively stuck in my victim mentality, I decided the only thing I could do was to throw myself deep into my business and ignore my true feelings. When faced with a problem, I would respond with *"I'm fine"* because I didn't have the strength or courage to admit the truth that I was secretly dying inside.

I would say to my husband, *"Everything will work out"* and *"I'll be rich, DON'T worry!"* But inside, I was screaming for help as I had no idea where to turn, causing me to react in explosive states of anger. I would push people away by rejecting love, support and guidance as I continued to feel ever so lonely.

My negative inner world was projecting even deeper into my current reality. It affected my loved ones and no matter how much I tried to avoid the problem, I knew deep down that I wasn't right in my head, I didn't feel right in my heart and I definitely did not feel good in my physical body.

My boys at the time needed their mum and all I cared about was building my business and ignored their needs. One morning, my husband said, *'You say hello to your phone, before you even kiss me good morning!'* I laughed it off, thinking he was being funny, but little did I know that this was a clear message to **Wake THE 'F' UP!**

We were both arguing so much that one day, he decided to pack his bag.

"I've had enough. I am not living in a relationship like this!"

We had a massive argument, I screamed and shouted and literally behaved in a state which would have required an exorcist! I burst into tears and begged him not to go, as I honestly had no idea what was wrong with me. This was the point in my life where I truly surrendered and acknowledged that I needed help and my personal development journey began. It also showed me how much my husband loved me, because he had in fact tricked me by carrying an empty bag; he was only going to his mum's! *The bugger!*

∞

I began to invest in myself and started my journey of self-development because not only did I know that there was emotional pain to release and that I had to overcome whatever this thing was inside of me, but I also needed to be a success. I noticed this recurring pattern within my business, where one minute I would flourish and then I would feel like I was failing. No matter how much I applied the morning routines and evening meditations, reading the affirmations and buying the deep hypnosis audios to transform my mind - NOTHING WAS DEEPLY WORKING.

Inside I felt awful, and outside my life felt like a rollercoaster.

I worked with several coaches, from spirituality to mindset, and it did help a little. I even worked with people who called themselves coaches but in fact, weren't all that to be honest and felt like they just wanted my money. I do believe each coach was sent to me for a reason as I learned a lot from them that was right for my journey and also what wasn't because there was still something inside that didn't feel right.

Instead of trying to understand myself and the reason this was happening, I decided to continue to ignore it and brush everything under the carpet until 2017 when everything changed.

With 3 collapsed MLM businesses and unable to hold a part time job, I met this coach who advised me that I should seriously consider coaching. I was so in love with network marketing that I couldn't dream of doing anything else. I wasn't achieving the levels of success that I deeply craved and my income was at an all-time low so I decided to put my faith and trust into this message that this was to be my next step. It was time for another change and **I HAD OFFICIALLY BECOME A COACH.**

∞

After a few months of coaching for free, as I had no idea how to make money without speaking to women for hours on the phone, I was like, "**RIGHT!** *I need to make some cash FAST,*" and I realised that in order to succeed, I needed help and guidance to build a business. The women who kept reaching out to me required mindset help and I had no idea how I could help them on a deeper level. I knew there was something more but I just didn't know what it was. I had a part time job at the time and I decided to hand in my notice in January 2018 and focus everything into my coaching career. This was a huge decision for me as I always had a back-up plan.

Little did I know, the reason all this had happened was because I was aligning, reconditioning, and rewiring my entire being to become the best version of me and that I had, in fact, *found my purpose.*

∞

Δ JOURNAL PROMPT Δ

It's time for you to grab your journals and reflect on the following questions:

- *What is the story you are telling yourself about your life today? Is it positive, negative or both?*
- *What emotions do you feel you are currently experiencing and how does it affect your life?*
- *Do you feel perhaps you could be avoiding something in your life that requires attention?*
- *Is there a part of you that feels like something is missing? If so, what do you think it could be?*
- *What do you feel you would need to face, to help you move forward?*
- *Why do you believe that you are here and what do you feel could be your purpose?*

Take some time to reflect on these questions, and remember, there is no right or wrong answer, just whatever feels right for you.

∞

WHAT ARE YOU DOING, THAT YOU ACTUALLY ENJOY DOING, THAT YOU REALLY DON'T WANT TO DO?

∞

Bit of a mind-boggling question, don't you think?

This is a question I ask every single client when they first jump on a call with me. It's about unlocking the deep-rooted block that causes them to avoid taking action, lack belief in themselves and constantly make excuses.

You are not a victim. You are not a problem.

You are a victor and the solution to everything. It's about awakening what you are doing, that you really don't want to do and understanding why.

When it comes to change, we as humans do not particularly enjoy it which is why most people feel stuck. Any habits we have and behaviours we exhibit are based on the conditioning and programming we have had instilled from the outside world and experienced through repetitive action. When we attempt to do things in a different way, we find it difficult to do so because we don't know how to approach it any differently. Which is why, if you have a habit that you don't want to do, you actually DO enjoy doing it because the habit has been so deeply integrated that you continue to do it without even knowing that in fact, you enjoy it. This my friend is called the comfort zone.

You could potentially be reading this, and think, "*I do not enjoy doing the things that make me miserable! I WANT TO CHANGE.*" The thing is, if you didn't enjoy doing the thing that you don't like to do, then you would do more of what you do want to do, *wouldn't you?* Now more than ever, a lot of people use the term procrastination which *means to avoid something by postponing an action* and claim that they are just serial procrastinators.

I am sure you are someone who totally recognises when you procrastinate, yet you still don't understand why you do it, or even how it's sabotaging your levels of success, *do you?*

I remember when I first discovered the term procrastination and how I was a leading expert in it. I cried so much because I really believed that who I was, was all that I could ever be. I really believed that there was no hope and that I couldn't be healed or changed. I really believed that I was not good enough and that nothing would ever work out for me. But in fact, when we are faced with the reality of what isn't working, we begin to unlock clarity to what really works and the awakening in itself can be quite emotional.

Procrastination, through repetition, becomes a chronic habit like an addiction, which is why, unless you understand exactly why you are doing it and eliminate it from the root cause, then the habit will continuously surface into your life, unless you undress the problem at a subconscious level. We become distracted and search for something else to do, because we DON'T WANT TO DO WHAT WE REALLY WANT TO DO and therefore avoiding change at all costs. I, for one, used to feel extremely tired and would want to sleep for weeks!

Now, a little use of your imagination:

Imagine going into a dark alley. There are no lights, no sounds, no one around. It feels scary, right? More than likely, you are going to turn back around and go in the direction that feels a lot less scary and a lot more comfortable because it feels safe – correct?

This is exactly what procrastination is when you attempt to do something a lot less ordinary.

Deep within your unconscious mind, based on the experiences you have been through, you have created a self-limiting belief that causes you to procrastinate. By forcing yourself to take action, no matter how much you want to get it done, something inside of you STOPS you from doing it.

For example, you decide to attempt to take action by doing something productive towards building your business, that you most probably haven't done before but you know it could help. No matter how much you push yourself, **YOU FEEL AS IF YOU CANNOT DO IT.**

The mental, physical and emotional process goes a little something like this:

1. *You think of taking the action consciously.*
2. *The thought of acting, begins to stir deep emotions that you most probably didn't know existed unconsciously.*
3. *This emotion, being negative (anger, fear, sadness, guilt, shame etc.), projects a signal to your nervous system throughout your body.*
4. *This triggers a chemical reaction in the brain caused by your unconscious thoughts and begins to feel uncomfortable, so you pull yourself back from doing it.*

5. *You then bring yourself back to the comfort zone, and decide to do something else, so you no longer feel triggered.*
6. *You then feel frustrated that you didn't do it and blame something or someone for it.*

You continue to do nothing at all.

This is why I believe procrastination is one of the most powerful things to unlock as the problem is so much deeper. When you discover the reason and the cause as to why you don't do the thing you want to do, everything begins to change.

∞

THE PROBLEM IS NOT THE PROBLEM, IT'S SOMETHING DEEPER.

The process of feeling our emotions is necessary for our healing, but because of our conditioning and our protective ego, we resist them, block them, and ignore them causing us to feel as if we are being attacked all the time. This then in return causes us to feel less likely to take any inspired action in anything we want to do.

Can you see how the emotional connection to procrastination holds you back?

It doesn't have anything to do with NOT achieving the results you desire; it's because deep down inside of you there is a root that requires plucking and the constant reactive behaviour to the outside world, is forcing you to ignore the deep feelings inside as to why you do the things you do.

For example, I had a client who came to me as she decided she wanted to work on her money mindset and enrolled on my Unlock Your Money Block® six-week one-on-one package.

On her intake form, she sent me a three-page answer of all the negative emotions and self-limiting beliefs she felt were preventing her from living an abundant life. Upon her first session, I had this urge to ask her, ***"Why are you so hard on yourself?"*** This triggered a memory in her mind and she went on to tell me about the time when she was five years old and had a major operation to remove a cyst from her brain. The doctors advised that she in herself would be fine however in a social setting and around others, she will not be able to communicate with others effectively. She then replied,

"I just feel so limited."

And there it was. Her money block was unleashed.

It had nothing to do with not feeling good enough, or guilty about spending and investing money, as she had originally told me. It was, in fact, her belief that she was limited and therefore money was limited. I kid you not, she burst into laughter, and her face was glowing with energy as if that switch had just turned on and she realised that in fact, the problem was a lot deeper.

A few weeks later, we removed the limiting belief and replaced it with *I am limitless*, as this is what she wanted to believe. Her breakthrough was just incredible. She realised how much this belief was preventing her from moving forward and holding her back in fear unable to make any trusted decisions. I asked her a few weeks after the session how she now felt, and her response was *"I just don't feel like thinking or worrying about the future anymore. I didn't even realise how much I did that and now I just feel more present and calmer."*

Her physiology, presence and energy had a complete shift which has now allowed her to be back in control of herself and her life. That's the power of releasing deep rooted blocks when you truly understand the root of it all and the reason why everything always starts, continues and evolves within you.

∞

△ JOURNAL PROMPT △

You can do whatever you put your mind to when you first understand who you truly are.

Grab your journals and reflect on the following so you can ease from miss procrastinator to miss motivator!

- *Do you believe you are a procrastinator? If so, why do you believe you are?*
- *How does it make you feel when you procrastinate?*
- *As you think of doing something new, what emotions come up for you?*
- *How does this impact your physical body?*
- *What kind of excuses do you make when it comes to taking inspired action?*
- *What do you believe could be the cause of this chronic habit?*
- *How do you feel now, after answering these questions?*

Please avoid forcing yourself to do anything you don't want to do without first understanding why you don't do it in the first place. Whatever the problem is that you are facing right now, it's about first understanding why you do it, and what you would have to do instead if this problem disappeared.

Now I want you to ask yourself:

"What is it that I currently do, that I seem to enjoy doing a lot, that I don't really want to do? And what would I be doing instead?"

Take your time on this one and answer as honestly as you can - trust yourself.

YOU CAN HAVE, BE AND DO WHATEVER YOU WANT - WHAT'S STOPPING YOU?

∞

HELLO EGO

Have you ever been told to hush that inner critic? Ignore the voices in your head? Just get on with it?

Perhaps you feel that you always know what's right for you, that no one knows you and if anyone tells you off, you instantly feel the need to defend yourself whilst thinking *hang on, why is everyone picking on me!?*

When I first became a coach, I remember feeling as if **I knew it all**. I couldn't ask for help because I deeply believed that I was invincible and therefore, uncoachable. My huge defensive ego was seriously in my way which caused major discomfort in my ability to make decisions with flourishing results.

The ego, believe it or not, is NOT your enemy. It feels like a voice inside you, which I believe protects you - not attacks you. Because of the experiences you have been through, albeit negative or positive, it's the voice that will tell you what you can and cannot do, preventing you from trusting yourself, because things in the past didn't work out the way you had hoped. It doesn't want you to get hurt again, and therefore steps in to protect you from making the same mistake whilst preventing you from asking for any help, even though you seek it.

Now, as a master coach in NLP, Time Line Therapy®, and Hypnotherapy, I dedicate my life to excelling in the work of the mind, the inner work, the mindset stuff; so, when it came to learning about the ego, especially when I was studying for my Montessori Diploma, I was fascinated.

Maria Montessori, the founder and creator of Montessori education, was a profound and phenomenal lady of this world. Her ethos was based on *following the child,* where adults through observations can create an environment that would allow the child to learn in a way that feels right for them. Instead of forcing them to do things because they have to, it was more about creating habits that allows them to auto correct themselves without the need of correction from an adult. This not only allowed the child to expand their knowledge and understanding of their world through their own eyes, but it also allowed them to form high levels of self-discipline from within by trusting their decisions and choices and by becoming confident in all that they do.

She also said that;

 "the hand is the pathway to the brain,"

My most favourite sentence that I had ever heard as it really helped me to understand that everything we touch, we absorb and therefore train our brains to create positive habits.

Through repetition, a child can learn and master new skills to help them throughout their life into adulthood. She believed in the individuality of each child rather than labelling them with a disorder if they didn't conform to society's expectation. By creating a prepared environment, we as adults can guide children to learn consciously and therefore create unconscious habits.

Isn't this just fascinating? I am so glad this was my first experience in understanding the mind because it not only helped me to become a better parent, but it also helped me guide my children to who they are today.

So knowing that the mind develops from as early as in the womb and throughout the early years, why is it that women in their thirties, forties and onwards, *(I say this age as this is the age of the women I tend to work with,)* suffer now, more than ever with imposter syndrome, sabotaging themselves with increased limitations? Why is it that they work on their minds ALL THE TIME, yet nothing changes?

WHEN YOU CHANGE THE WAY YOU LOOK AT THINGS, THE THINGS YOU LOOK AT CHANGE, right?

It's like the more you work on yourself, the more you feel overwhelmed, anxious and stressed and you keep burning out. It's as if there is no middle ground or balance, and instead of actually paying attention to what the ego is telling you and why, *as it isn't always being mean,* you ignore it, blame yourself to avoid facing the problem and seek external validation. This is because you are unable to tap into your inner voice - **the real you.**

Even though the ego speaks negatively and it feels better to avoid the message, if you listen to the feeling and understand where it started, you are far more able to effectively heal the wound. *Imagine how it could talk to you instead?*

The inner critic, the negative nancy, or whatever you want to call it, is just talking to you from experience. Your perception of the world is all based around your past events which has conditioned your ego to be the way that it is. This is why you feel as if you cannot do certain things that you want to do. It's not your fault, life's fault or anyone else's fault. It's just programming in the unconscious part of you that can be reprogrammed at any point in your life and why I deeply believe that the mind-work at the unconscious level requires deep healing, without having to relive the past.

When you seriously master your thoughts, feelings and emotions you can finally heal the wounded voice, and everything really does change as you reconnect to you.

∞

THE VICTIM MENTALITY

"Resistance is the first step to change. When you overcome it, everything flows."

Do you ever find yourself saying these things?

THE CHILDREN MADE ME LATE!

THE DRIVER CUT ME UP AND RUINED MY DAY!

IT'S THE MOON'S FAULT I'M IN A SHITTY MOOD!

ON NO! NOT ANOTHER RETROGRADE!

I HATE MY LIFE!

Hand on heart, I was the biggest victim on the planet. I really felt that everything and anything always went wrong for me, leaving me in tears ALL THE TIME. I would blame the drivers on the road, the children, the lack of success, my entire life, and even the moon!

As much as the moon and other events in your life can impact your energy, moods, and emotions, it's NOT the MAIN reason as to why you feel triggered and so negative and everything else under the sun! *(Funny how we always use planets to describe things).*

The truth is, well, the REASON is you.

Now I am not a woo-woo type of girl, but you cannot deny the energy or the impact of the moon. There has been research throughout the years how the moon's magnetic impact seems to heighten certain moods around the lunar phase cycle. Apparently, we turn into reckless, incapable human beings! I admit, during the new moon, I do feel tired or exhausted and can feel a bit disruptive at times. However for most, life feels a lot more painful to face and the blame game then begins. But it's not the moon's fault if I/you/we act like a complete dick or if something goes wrong; It's not the moon's fault if I snap at the kids! It's not as if the moon plans to sabotage us every month, or twice a month for most, like a muvva-luvvin period and say,

"Hey you! You're getting on my tits! I'm going to turn you into a pain in the ass!"

I mean, we are happy when the sun is beaming, but not when it's hiding behind the clouds and the next thing you know, we got S.A.D!

For me, I realised before my coaching process of releasing and reframing, that I did tend to become overly emotional around the moon phases; however, I also knew that I was holding onto a lot of pain.

As humans, in the physical form, we believe that there is always something that causes us to feel in a particular way. Truthfully, it's just an excuse to avoid change. Yes, there will always be something as the cause, but the effect - *how we react/respond* - will always be our responsibility.

Instead, the victim mentality comes into full throttle and we start to blame people and experiences as to why we feel the way we do. I, for one, suffered tremendous amounts of abuse as a child, and although it affected my mind and my life, I couldn't blame it any longer and I had to work deep down to start shifting from reactive to responsive.

When we are the victor, we accept responsibility and shift from effect to cause and are thereby no longer consumed by outside effect. We accept what the truth really is and CHOOSE to respond in a better way, without being consumed with negativity.

If you are constantly blaming SOMETHING for your behaviour, you're in the VICTIM mode because the ability to accept responsibility for your moods and feelings isn't possible because you don't know how to move through it.

So, how do we clear these blockages that prevent us from accepting responsibility?

You need to feel, release and access the emotions at a cellular level.

∞

Every time I work with a new client they feel so excited, *I mean so pumped*, that they message me and tell me how ready they are to make the change. Me being me, intuitively attune into the client's energy and as soon as women sign the dotted line, I would say about 45% of the women, they will cancel their first session and want to reschedule it because they become poorly, or something will come up that prevents them from beginning their journey of transformation.

Life gets in the way and all the excuses come up.

Funnily enough, a client asked me yesterday if she could take a break.

I replied nope, see you tomorrow!

Why?

Because the journey of transformation requires consistency, a willingness to change and a commitment to growth. It will require you to think less victim and feel more victorious. When you are not used to this kind of shift, the unconscious mind and ego work together to pull you back and keep you in the victim mentality because the negative emotions you experience are coming from inside of you and have always been there. If you have *tried* to work on your mindset and the old patterns of behaviour, which you THOUGHT you had released still haven't gone, then you have to understand that you have been thinking, feeling and behaving in the same way for decades and it will require some seriously deep rewiring if you ever want to let it all go.

To integrate the new, this will require some time and adjustment which means taking care of yourself to allow integration to process, as you recondition and deeply heal your subconscious mind.

It goes much deeper beyond the sun, the moon, and the stars –
IT'S YOU.

As emotional beings, your emotional intelligence requires you to understand why you act and think the way you do by increasing your levels of emotional awareness and emotional regulation. You have to go through a process to get to this place, like a personality transformation and when you do, you literally stand, see, feel, act and speak like never before.

Through accomplishing this myself, I can't even describe how incredible the shift was. It was as if I could finally live moment by moment rather than day by day. So much has shifted in my life, my mind, my body, my spirit, my business, my relationships, EVERYTHING, because life isn't a race or to be lived in fear of the outcome – it's supposed to be an adventure.

No one has the right to dictate your moods; only you can manage your emotions and know how to handle any challenge. When you understand how to motivate yourself, even on an off day, you feel less guilt about taking time out for yourself.

It's about tapping into yourself. THE REAL YOU.

The moon is the moon - it disappears every new moon phase and reappears every full moon phase. I do like the spiritual activity behind it such as the releasing, and setting intentions, I mean, I got married on a new moon! So, things like this can be used to your advantage.

But don't blame the moon for your behaviour or anything else.

Start to understand yourself and begin to take back control of you and your emotions by acknowledging your deep pains as to why you feel the way you do, because that's what's *really* holding you back – not your kids, or the driver cutting you up, or even THE MOON. *It's far too pretty.*

If the problem started within, then the solution is also there too.

If you go to my website, www.samevansglobal.com, I have an exclusive complimentary training to help you understand why you procrastinate and how to get totally motivated. Be sure to check it out!

Δ JOURNAL PROMPT Δ

"When we learn to accept the voice and explain that we are in control, we begin to allow room for shifts and breakthroughs."

I remember when my inner voice was overtaking everything in my life, until one day, I just exploded. I had enough of feeling this way, so I screamed out silently:

"FUCK OFF MIND! LISTEN - I GOT YOU! TRUST ME, PLEASE! I LOVE YOU. I CAN DO THIS."

(I know, pretty drastic but I had no choice)! My inner voice was driving me insane, so I finally took back control of my mind and began my own healing journey as my ego realised I was not messing around!

It's time for you to listen to your ego. Grab your journal, sit at your desk, take a few deep breaths.

- *I want you to ask yourself out loud, "Ego, what are you telling me?" and just listen for a minute.*
- *Write down what it told you.*
- *Why does it feel so scared and wounded?*
- *What is it protecting you from?*
- *Why is it preventing you from taking action and moving forward?*
- *How has it impacted your life keeping you in this place of fear?*
- *How would life change for you if you healed it?*
- *What could you now do to reconnect with your inner voice and heal your ego?*

Once this is done, place your hand on your heart, and repeat out loud:

"Ego, I love you. I got you. Trust me. We are safe."

AND JUST BREATHE.

EMOTIONAL INTELLIGENCE 2.0

∞

Everyone seems to be talking about emotional intelligence lately, *don't you think?* I know it was most certainly NOT something I completely understood in the past, which is why I took many courses to understand it, apply it, live it and breathe it by becoming a TTi UK approved practitioner and an EQ practitioner.

When we understand our emotions, we become far more able to understand ourselves, and therefore behave in a calmer way where we can achieve more of what we want.

This is why in this chapter, I am going to explain to you in the simplest way possible, what it is, how it affects you, how it affected me and what it can do for you in terms of money, success and how to simply be as a human on this planet, when you improve it *(no matter how old you are)*.

It's not just about knowing your emotions, it's much deeper. As you begin to deeply understand your current levels of emotional intelligence and the empowering and vital role it plays, you will know that there is always time to improve it when it comes to mastering yourself.

I remember one day, my youngest was oogling at me, as in smiling, dribbling, staring, and he couldn't take his eyes off me. It actually made me feel really uncomfortable, so I asked my hubby; "*BABE! He's really staring at me, and I don't know why? I know it sounds crazy, but I feel like he's perving on me!*"

WHAT THE EFF!

How could I even feel that way about my baby!? My hubby laughed and replied,

"*No Sam! He is looking at you with love.* **He loves you.**"

My jaw dropped in shock because despite being married to the man of my dreams with two beautiful boys and having everything I always wanted, I really had no idea what true love was, until that moment.

I was so upset and annoyed at myself because I really didn't know how to be a mum. I was hell bent on becoming the perfect mum, the perfect wife, the perfect Sam, to look good, (like I did before I had children), to be that fun time Sammy but instead, I felt more and more isolated, trapped in my mind and completely disconnected from my true self as I seriously lacked the ability to understand my own emotions and how to accept other people's emotions as well.

My darkness consumed my very existence with the inability to embrace the light that was dying to come out, which is why I am so grateful for my coaching journey because as much as I serve others, it was a massive service to me and my growth.

For the record, emotional intelligence is also known as Emotional Quotient and for the rest of this chapter, I'll be referring to it as EQ.

∞

IT'S NOT JUST ABOUT KNOWLEDGE

"Emotional intelligence is the single biggest predictor of performance in the workplace and the strongest driver of leadership and personal excellence."
(Forbes Magazine)

When it comes to managing and increasing your EQ, it's generally considered to comprise four pillars. These are, awareness of your own emotions, how to manage your emotions, understanding the emotions of others, and how to influence other people's emotions as well and can be measured with a personalised EQ assessment.

Within a year of taking my first EQ assessment, I had a 900% increase in my salary as I was able to understand myself at a whole new level and therefore apply my knowledge in a far more effective way thus achieving better results.

They used to say that it was all about the IQ for anyone to ever be super successful.

KNOWLEDGE IS POWER!

Yes, it does help, but if you are unable to apply that knowledge into your life due to fears and doubts, and for you to seriously tap into and embody your knowledge, you will need to increase your levels of EQ.

Your IQ can be the same at fifteen years of age and fifty years of age. However, when you increase your EQ, you start to effectively create more success in all areas of your life as you tap into your

IQ at a whole new level. You improve your mental health and wellbeing, gain better performance in all that you do, have loving and improved relationships, as you tap into your inner light simply by unlocking your potential.

Growing up as a child at school, I never really understood things quickly. It would take me years to comprehend and understand any topics mentally as I found it so difficult. Even when I passed my Montessori Diploma, it wasn't until the day before my final exam that I finally was able to understand Maria's ethos behind her education. I was great at remembering, but understanding and reflecting - *not really my best power!* I literally was winging it!

If I had the mindset I have now back at school, I would have been an A+ student but then if I hadn't gone through the journey I have, then I most probably wouldn't even be here writing this book, because *everything happens for a reason!*

(By the way, if you go to my website, I have an EQ test to help you start your own journey of self-discovery under offers).

∞

I'M SO EMOTIONAL!

Our wellbeing is our mental, physical, spiritual and emotional health and if any of the areas are not 100%, then this is seen as being out of alignment. To feel whole is to think good thoughts, feel good and to trust yourself by listening to your intuition and taking care of your human body. I'm not saying it's about ignoring the emotions - *of course not!* You have to feel both highs and lows because without the lows, how can you ever know what a high *feels* like, right?

When you understand why you think the way you do, you can understand why you feel the way you do. When you understand how you feel, you can then improve, shift or change the way that you react without relying on the little voice inside your head that seems to cause you to react in a particular way, *even if you don't want to*. This is why I always say, (as learned at practitioner level in NLP), that **people are not their behaviours** – they are just living in a world that feels safe to them, responding the only way they know how, based on their own experiences.

Our emotions are very much interlinked with our personalities as we are described based on our feelings i.e. bubbly, snappy, aggressive, or even quiet. If emotions are what we feel and personality is how we act, our behaviour is therefore how we respond and our overall wellbeing is how we are as a human, which is why most people don't even know why they act the way they do and just feel it's just how they are.

Perhaps you cry for no reason, without even knowing why you do, and you tell yourself that you are just a crier - it's just who you are.

I used to tell everyone I was tiny tears, as I would cry over everything. But being emotional does not mean you are an overly emotional person; it's a good sign that you are releasing the toxins from your body and that there is something a lot deeper that requires healing.

For example, a client recalled a memory with an ex-partner, where she felt unworthy. Her body went into fear, doubt and not feeling good enough which reflected in her physiology because deep down, she believed that she wasn't worthy enough to be in a relationship. This traumatic experience sent a shock message to her nervous system, which caused her body to respond via fight, flight or freeze mode, making her feel really uncomfortable. This is why most people are so defensive or overly emotional because the memories stored in the deep subconscious mind are triggering their very existence.

Feeling as if you are stuck and stagnant in the negative emotions is damaging for the physical body as it harms the body by creating illnesses, stress and depression, and in some cases, it can cause death. When you understand how you are, reprogramme the mind, and pay attention to your emotions by taking care of yourself, you, in turn, change the way you feel and the way you behave in the world. You start to act, think and feel differently, as if you have had a personality transplant. You become more responsive than reactive and start to attract even more of what you want, as opposed to what you don't want. You communicate with others far better; you start to respond to certain areas in your life differently as you begin to feel a lot more positive inside and raise your levels of self-awareness.

∞

SELF AWARENESS

My entire life I spent pleasing people. I just wanted to fit in with the latest crowd, have the man of my dreams, be the best and most perfect living being on this earth, just so that I could say *I DID IT*. As I began to work for myself, I genuinely did want to make an impact, to leave a legacy for my children and know that my work has had a major impact on this earth. But I wasn't listening to my emotional needs as I really didn't know myself. I would constantly feel sorry for myself, wallowing in self-pity because I wasn't getting the results I wanted fast enough and I had no idea what was causing me to feel this way.

My body was suffering. My heart was broken. My spirit was sad.

To seriously understand and improve yourself, self-awareness is a very powerful way to unlock any deep-rooted limiting beliefs and the level of pain you are potentially living in. By intuitively listening to yourself, your thoughts and addressing your feelings by becoming aware of your strengths and weaknesses, you can effectively learn how to face any difficult situation because you know yourself to a T.

It's about understanding why you think and feel the way you do – not just noticing it.

I know you are self-aware. We all are. We know when we feel hurt, frustrated and annoyed. We know when we are happy and joyful. We, as humans, are more self-aware than we give ourselves credit for because if we can find a problem, we can create a solution too.

Increasing your levels of self-awareness requires you to break the old ways to move through into the new. Nothing else will cut it, unless you do the deep integration of a new way of thinking, feeling and behaving. It's not about going one step forward, ten steps back anymore. It's about understanding who you are now so you can energetically align your heart, mind and spirit as one.

It's about doing the things when you think you can't - **because you can.**

It's about leaving what you knew before and **giving yourself permission to move.**

It's about **desiring to change and committing to doing the things you need to do and being ready** for some ground work.

And most importantly, **it's about allowing your emotions to surface.**

It's so possible: and when you do, your potential is waiting for you.

∞

SELF-REGULATION

Once you begin to raise your levels of self-awareness, it's about learning how to control your thoughts and feelings with the ability to get out of any mental and emotional ruts that you do not feel aligned to, as you begin to trust the decisions that you make.

Someone once asked me to write in 100 words what makes me happy and I was over the moon that I could do this, because once upon a time, I JUST COULDN'T.

Is this something that you say to yourself, *"I wish I could be happy?"*

I wish I was happy all the time.

I wish I could have the answers to all of my problems.

I wish I could have a shit tonne of money.

I wish I could be successful.

I wish I could meet the man of my dreams.

I wish I could fucking have it all!

I hate to break it to you, it's not the wishes that come

true - it's your increased belief in yourself that anything is possible, and then achieving it.

Happiness is a feeling - an emotion. It's a state and a choice that I make very clear to my clients that only they can choose to be happy. Believe it or not, when we get frustrated or fearful, this again is also a choice, but we as humans absorb negativity a thousand times faster than positivity, which is why we feel more consumed with negativity than positivity because we have no idea how to tap into that joyful emotion.

Most people tend to search for external sources of validation to be happy. But nothing can make you feel happy unless you feel happiness from within. It comes from when you love yourself whole, value yourself and appreciate everything in your life, for what you have achieved and made. **Anything else is a bonus**.

When we come from a place of lack, we lack gratitude, appreciation and love for the things that we have in our lives. If the problem exists within you, OWN IT because the solution exists within you too.

Want more good vibes!?

Start feeling it. Thinking it. Believing it.

You have the power in you to make anything happen.

Whenever I do reach a stage of lack, I tend to pause, reflect and ask myself, ***"Why Am I Snappy?"*** Not *Why am I NOT happy? WHY AM I SNAPPING?* It's about deeply understanding why I do the things I do and what I can do to overcome it by regulating my own emotions.

If the mind has been conditioned to think, feel and behave in a particular way, it's not about affirming *I'M HAPPY* and then expecting roses to flush out of your ass! It's about gently moving from the current state to the desired state, with growth and understanding, so if you ever feel this way again, you know EXACTLY WHAT TO DO.

Regulating your emotions is essential in every area of your life, not just for your loved ones or for success, but for your mental and emotional wellbeing because you are the only one in charge of you.

I do love it when clients tell me how happy they now feel and how in control they feel of their emotions, simply because they were able to release the trapped negative emotions from their mind and bodies. It just sings to my soul!

∞

SOCIAL AWARENESS

Social awareness is exactly like self-awareness but instead, you can effectively read the emotional makeup of other people. It's about understanding empathy, how well you get along with people, and how others perceive you socially. Now this doesn't mean worrying about other people's opinions! It's about how you express yourself effectively to create success, friendships and deep and meaningful relationships.

I had so many different types of friends in my life, *but were they really friends?* I guess they were in some respect, but when I really needed them, they were not there. I most certainly was not a breeze in the park and perhaps not the greatest friend at all. I was so consumed with drugs and living in the victim mentality as all I cared about was myself.

It's not as if we were ever educated on the mind or how the past controls our present, were we?

I struggled a lot with men and even with my family, unable to connect deeply and create meaningful relationships because I just felt as if everyone was always judging me. I always felt that I gave more than I received. I mean, no one taught me how to be a girl-friend, a friend, a wife, or a mother. I never had best friends as such, or ones that stuck around for long and I never ever had anyone who really truly understood me, until I met my husband. He was the one that was sent to me, upon request, and trans-formed my perception because boy, I was a tough nut to crack!

When it comes to empathy, which means *how you experience someone else's feelings,* this comes from the German term *Einfühlung,* or *'feeling into.'* It requires an emotional component of really feeling what the other person is feeling by putting yourself in their shoes in order to understand why they feel the way they do, which is exactly what I do in my coaching practice. Sympathy, however, is more about feeling sorry for someone, or pity for them, and not being able to understand specifically how to connect to them because you cannot understand what they are feeling. It's more cognitive in nature and keeps a certain distance.

I used to feel sorry for absolutely anyone, especially when I became a coach as I would offer discount services, putting high hopes that everything would financially work out. I would feel petrified to ask for the fee because I lacked belief in myself and my services and I would then go on to offer free coaching which would leave me feeling lethargic and exhausted. But it's not about pleasing people, or even how you effectively run a business; It's about setting clear boundaries, knowing what you deserve and feeling confident in everything you do without impacting your levels of energy.

Once you master yourself, you master your surroundings without the need to take on the world of other people's problems, because you know what's important to you.

∞

SOCIAL REGULATION

The final part of mastering your EQ is learning how to be around other people by understanding other people's emotions. It's not just about speaking; it's about being aware of their body language and then deeply understanding the other person by genuinely being interested in their thoughts, feelings and listening to them.

When we are working with other people, the important factor to remember is how we react to how they behave. Having a high level of EQ in this context basically means, instead of being overly reactive, we create better responses instead, *kinda like what I spoke about in the intro, when I showed a client her reflection and she didn't respond well to it.* I had to hold that space for her by showing an understanding of where she was right then, listening to how she was feeling and how I could help her resolve her problems. When you understand others, you also understand yourself without feeling triggered or vulnerable which could, in turn, damage the relationship with the other person.

REMEMBER, PEOPLE ARE NOT THEIR BEHAVIOURS!

Some people may react in a way that could trigger us or cause us to alarm certain emotions that we may not have dealt with, but if we master ourselves, our emotions and how we are with others, we have a far better and more effective way to influence others to change.

In 2018, a time when I was heavily on drugs, an ex-friend was crying on my sofa, and all I cared about was going to sleep. I had no idea of what was happening around me because I was so into myself, instead of realising that she needed me. I was so high on drugs and hadn't slept for two days, which most probably didn't help and caused me to create a major problem with my friends and eventually to be kicked out of the group. Perhaps if I paid more attention, then we would still be friends? Or did everything happen for a reason? WHO KNOWS? The point is, I should have been more attentive and aware that she needed me.

This is why building relationships is another high level of EQ to create meaningful connections, rapport, trust and empowering relationships.

I really do believe that in order to master your EQ, to deeply understand what is holding you back, and to understand why you do the thing you love to do *(that you don't want to)*, you have to take a look in the mirror, accept who you are NOW so that you can have, be and do everything you want, simply by understanding the negative, before you put your positive polly pants on and take on the world.

SAM EVANS

∞

Δ JOURNAL PROMPT Δ

Grab your journals - it's time to reflect and get super specific!

Remember, everyone starts somewhere.

There is no right or wrong answer, just be open and ready to accept new ways of managing yourself, for yourself and for others.

∞

- *When you feel positive, what happens to you and how does this help you in your day-to-day life?*
- *When you feel negative, what happens to you and how do you currently react/respond to a challenge?*
- *How do you currently feel about your decision-making ability?*
- *What are your current relationships like with family, friends and clients or the opposite sex?*
- *Do you feel you are a good listener?*
- *Do you feel you are too empathetic? If so, how does this impact you?*
- *What have you discovered about yourself when it comes to emotional intelligence?*

∞

Place your hand on your heart, and repeat out loud:

"It's safe for me to be. I accept who I am. I am ready."

PART II
IMPLEMENTATION

Become you.

Before you state there is nothing to do, before you declare there is no point, before you decide you're gonna wait until this is over,

ASK YOURSELF, IS THIS WHAT YOU WOULD DO IF THIS WAS YOUR LAST LIVING DAY ON EARTH?

Tomorrow is today's action without yesterday's pain.

What you think you know:

That this is just life, and nothing will ever change.

What you require to know:

Your conditioning is seriously sabotaging your life.

What you don't know:

Is how to become more present IN THE NOW.

BYE-BYE EXCUSES!

I know you are aware and I know you know your worth.
I know how much it means to you to make a difference, an impact to ripple effect your power on this earth in this lifetime.
I also know there is resistance.
Resistance to accept who you are.
Resistance to believe you are good enough.
Resistance to owning the truth that lies within, caused by your subconscious, unconsciously controlling
Every thought. Every feeling. Every move.
The endless battles inside are driving you crazy.
But now it's time.
It's time to allow the energetic flow of ease to become a daily part of your routine.
It's time to master your entire being and trust yourself in everything you do.
*It's time to take control because the past **doesn't** have to dictate your present any longer."*

SELF ACTUALISATION

∞

IT'S SO HARD TO BE ME

I remember when I used to watch all these thriving millionaires online and wonder,

how the heck do they do it all?

They run a business, take care of their children and family, and still have time to jet set across the globe. *There is no way that I could live a life like that*, or so I thought.

Like most, I was advised to do the things that I said that I would NEVER DO within my businesses, (making calls, DM's, pitching BLURGH!) which meant I had to step out of my comfort zone and face my inner critic and do something new.

No matter how much I TRIED to apply new techniques or methods into any of my businesses, I just kept making excuses to avoid stepping outside my zone of comfort and felt sick in the pit of my stomach. I just couldn't bring myself to do the things I had never done or actually wanted to do.

We've been told our entire lives that we *have to work hard* to get good at anything, so no wonder we feel overwhelmed, uncertain and doubtful at ever achieving the results that we deeply want. The peer pressure from the outside world causes major disturbance to our inner world, triggering limiting beliefs, causing us to feel ANXIOUS and ANNOYED and left wondering, ***will I ever just be normal?***

Despite feeling the fears and doubts from within, you recognise that by having a bullet-proof mindset, you can and will BE FREE!

You apply the LOA into your lives, affirm in the mirror that everything is freakin' wonderful! You consistently post positivity everywhere, on your social media sites, pretending that you are living the life of luxury when deep down you feel that you are not. You write in your gratitude journal repeating over and over how grateful you are, despite feeling completely miserable, but you see how others are succeeding by applying the law, so you think to yourself, that it could possibly work for you too.

"THIS IS IT! I'M GOING TO BE A SUCCESS! If they can - I CAN!"

But then, reality hits!

What if I don't get any clients/customers?

What if I don't make any money?

What if no one takes me seriously? What if it doesn't work out?

WHAT IF I FAIL?

By wanting to take action, and getting uncomfortable, this gut-wrenching feeling overrides your decision and ability to do so, causing you to feel that it wasn't the right thing to do and then you worry what other people may think. **Not what you think** – what others might say, especially if you do something that isn't normal to them.

The little voice creeps in and tells you:

"YOU ARE A FAILURE."

The ego takes over, blocking your ability to listen to your true inner voice that actually wants you to be ok. It wants you to gain enjoyment and satisfaction out of the present moment and in everything you do. But because you are seeking validation externally, pushing the need to be FIXED, HEALED and BETTER, this then prevents you from being true to yourself, and therefore your ego and subconscious programming hold you back so that you don't feel the rejection.

How do you overcome yourself and become the best version of you, without the need to be fixed?

It's about understanding what you need in order to gain a sense of fulfilment in your life and being true to your desires as you reach your fullest potential, without making everything feel so freaking hard.

∞

JUST BE YOU

Becoming aware of your inner truths is your confirmation, saying *"YES this is me, this is how I feel, and I am no longer lying to myself anymore"* because you become true to yourself, open, honest and trust yourself as you recondition your current mindset. You step into your divine truth of who you really are – the real you. This is why becoming the authentic version of you feels difficult because of the constant brushing away of the problems and not facing them.

But why does becoming authentic feel so hard?

Everyone talks about being authentic and becoming the best version of yourself, and I get it. **I do.** Once upon a time, I remember when I believed that being abrupt and rude was just me and who I was, and if you didn't like it, **FUCK OFF**! *Yes, I do speak my truth, but it doesn't mean I can't be empathetic towards others.* Back then, I lacked empathy enormously by not being able to understand other people's feelings. I had no idea how to be me because I just wanted to be accepted. The more I tried to fit in, the harder it felt and the more rejection I faced with knockbacks at every given corner.

Forcing yourself to be positive isn't the answer. It's not about ignoring the problems you are currently worrying about and hoping they will magically disappear whilst you pretend you are happy, smiling as if there is no problem to solve; it's about recognising who you truly are NOW, to your inner core and understanding why you feel the way you do so that you can tap into you and become the best version of yourself.

This I feel is quite possibly the most challenging shift that anyone ever goes through. Instead of being stuck in the problem, you begin to uncover the solution as you begin to flow with ease, trust, and create belief in yourself; but because you are not used to it, you will want to go back to where you feel comfortable. However, as you evolve with unshakeable faith, you do naturally flow with happiness, joy and passion in everything you do with everyone you love as you transition into the best version of you.

Being in that energetic vibe encourages you to continue achieving more success in all areas of your life as you reach an energetic alignment to all that you are, and all that you have.

∞

3 A's

To become the best version of you I believe there are 3 A's to the authentic equation.

Firstly *awareness*.

It's about becoming super self-aware of who you are now.

We are all emotional beings and we have a choice on how we perceive ourselves, which means accepting our personalities, our behaviours, and most importantly, ourselves.

This is why it's crucial to improve your levels of emotional intelligence so that you can become aware of how you manage your emotions and how it impacts you, as well as others.

Secondly, *acceptance*.

Accepting yourself is accepting everything about you - period. It doesn't determine how you live your life or how you should be, it's just a part of your current makeup.

Without acceptance, acceptance to grow and a willingness to change, you will only hinder your ability to become more present. This is why I believe forgiveness is so important in the evolution process so that you can let go of the old and embrace the new.

Thirdly, *appreciation*.

This is vital. If we don't appreciate what we have, then how will we ever achieve more of what we want? It's about celebrating every single mistake, every single win, every single move we make, no matter how big or small. It's always going to be a step in the right direction, which is why to be in flow, now, it's about being so grateful for all that you have achieved, the lessons that you have learned and all that you are about to receive.

E V E R Y T H I N G.

∞

ACKNOWLEDGE

I remember sitting on the sofa crying my eyes out and feeling so sorry for myself in 2020 because I just felt like such a failure in my business. I had a chat with a good friend and she couldn't figure out why I felt this way.

"SAM you are the mindset queen? WHY IS THIS HAPPENING TO YOU?"

I had no idea myself, but I knew there was something I wasn't paying attention to. I felt this urge to enrol with a coach, *stimulating my need to be fixed as I had a serious course addiction.*

I had watched this coach help so many women on social media, reach income levels that I couldn't envision for myself. I signed up with a feeling of lack, it's not possible and uncertainty, which wasn't the right decision for me. Something deep was causing me problems and instead of making a trusted decision out of desire, I made a poor decision in a low vibe which wasn't a good move. However, at the time I didn't even care because I was so desperate to be *'fixed'* not knowing that there was another limiting belief appearing out of the woodworks.

I began the course and instantly I realised that IT WAS NOT FOR ME. I *thought perhaps it was me, perhaps it will get better, perhaps there is something missing?* I pushed through it but felt so misaligned as it went completely against my ethos, beliefs and strategies and I knew it wasn't helping.

I felt so triggered by this coach and I couldn't understand why. She seemed to be helping everyone else, *why not me?* I then felt a tremendous amount of guilt because I didn't know how to tell this coach that this program wasn't for me.

In the end, I decided to stand by my intuitive guide and acknowledge that this was not for me, and I left on good terms. What a relief that was.

This is the power of acknowledging; *especially when things do not feel right*.

I decided to work on myself to understand why I felt this need to be fixed. Using my tools, I dug a little deeper to break down what was going on and raise my awareness of why I felt this way and the emotions causing me pain. The emotions that came up for me were frustration, envy, shame, and guilt, all combined into one.

I began to recall a memory of when I was six years old, standing in the playground and no one wanted to play with me. There weren't many Indians at this school, and the other children were being *really mean* and shut me out.

I was trying to prove myself to them that I was just like them and that I could be a part of their crowd.

But why should I have to do that? Why was I trying so hard to fit in when they didn't approve certain aspects of me? And most importantly, why should I disapprove myself?

That's when I realised why I felt this way with this coach, and why I felt so triggered, because this event in my life allowed me to face another block that was causing me pain – **I WAS TRYING TO FIT IN!**

It made so much sense! The different crowds I stumbled from as a teenager; the inability to hold down a job longer than eighteen months; the need to be accepted by men, and to 'FIT IN.' I desperately had the habit of needing to be needed, and to be a part of something which is what I SEEKED from this coach:

I WAS SEEKING APPROVAL THAT I WAS GOOD
ENOUGH TO BE A SUCCESS.

But I am a part of something huge and I am good enough to do anything and everything. I'm a mum, a wife and a coach on a mission by the one and only with a power to serve those who need it – I just didn't realise it, until then.

The most empowering acknowledgement is, in fact, when you DON'T feel positive and instead address the negativity within. This is your ability to know how to handle yourself, how to react, how to motivate yourself and how you are socially and empathetically.

It's not just about being positive and hoping for a magical answer to appear; it's about having a deep sense of self-awareness to help you master your emotions by improving and mastering your EQ.

∞

ACCEPTANCE

When I realised what I felt and let it go, I had to deeply accept and admit that I had this need to be a part of something because if I'm honest, it was the hardest thing I ever had to confess to myself.

My entire life was based on fitting in, so I had to deeply break the old habit of being myself to make room for new habits and feelings. Once you recognise your core truths and become aware of your current perception, you accept *what is*.

Acceptance is more than accepting the good; it's also accepting the things that don't work. It can feel difficult because it's like admitting you were in the wrong in the first place and it feels uncomfortable, as if you failed. That doesn't mean it defines you, it's just a part of who you are right now and feeling like a failure doesn't mean it's final – it just means accepting something isn't working or feeling right, and that you can do so much better. You can do no wrong, it's whatever is right for you as you are always in the right place at the right time.

> *Where you are now is not where you will always be, but you are heading in the right direction.*

Knowing this will not only help you to understand and grow when it comes to facing those challenges, but to also know yourself at a whole new level.

> *Remember when I told you earlier about how I asked my husband the truth about me and why things kept happening?*

> ### *BECAUSE IT HURTS!*

The truth can hurt, and this is why it's vital to learn to accept your true feelings and surrender your doubts so that you can move forward with grace.

∞

APPRECIATION

Can you see how vital it is to change your unconscious programming?

It doesn't matter how hard you want something to work, your current way of living will continue to affect your entire life unless you begin to start feeding and reprogramming your subconscious mind.

This is why I just love journaling and working on myself, because when you reflect and become completely honest with yourself and are able to set yourself free from any limitations, you naturally begin to come from a place of gratitude which in turn, allows you to connect to your future desires.

I do believe that by having consistent routines of repetitive and positive daily habits, you support your subconscious programming if you want to change any aspect of your reality, *especially if you have never done it before.*

By having daily habits and routines that feel right for you, it not only helps you step into the person you desire to be, but you instantly begin to see positive changes in your life. Even by applying just ten minutes in the morning and ten minutes in the evening, when you can give yourself the time and space to tap in and listen to yourself, this will support your journey to wherever you desire to be with deep appreciation for yourself.

An attitude of gratitude is one of the most powerful tools you can use to achieve true success and why getting behind your analytical mind to create real and permanent change via repetition will reinforce the circuits in your brain to support the changes of how you think and feel every single day.

ACKNOWLEDGE WHO YOU ARE.

ACCEPT WHO YOU ARE TO BECOME.

APPRECIATE WHERE YOU ARE GOING.

AND BECOME THE REAL YOU IN THE NOW.

∞

Δ JOURNAL PROMPT Δ

Everything you need - You already have.
It exists beyond your fears, doubts and anxiety.

When you tap into your passion that fuels your purpose, listen to it, attune to it,
and become the real you.

Grab your journals! It's time to get to work!

- *What's in your life makes you feel comfortable?*
- *What's in your life makes you feel uncomfortable?*
- *As you think of your life at this moment, where are you now in relation to what you desire?*
- *What is working for you and what do you feel is not working for you in your life right now?*
- *What can you do now to get comfortable being uncomfortable?*
- *What do you feel stops you from reaching your potential and when you plateau, what happens? What stops you from moving forward?*
- *What emotions, both positive and negative, come up for you as you write about this?*
- *What can you now start appreciating in your life that everything is actually working out for you?*

Place your hand on your heart, and say out loud,

"It's safe to be me, I'm grateful that I am here, and I am ready for my next step!"

WHAT DO YOU WANT? NO, REALLY!

∞

OWN YOUR GODDAMN SELF!

Whatever the change is, IT'S MEANT TO BE - no matter how uncomfortable it will feel.

We go through life THINKING we know what we are supposed to do, WE KNOW what's right, we don't need to be told anything different because we KNOW IT ALL!

I was always chasing and searching for the right thing to help me because I was so ready to be free. What I didn't realise was HOW EXHAUSTING AND HOW HARD the mind work really is - because when you REFRAME, LET GO and MOVE FORWARD, you are totally transforming the mind from how you used to think to how you will think and actually, it's how you want to think.

You gotta be prepared to trust the process and know that deep down, this is going to help you achieve massive results based on whatever you truly desire and whatever you desire will earn you massive results when you take the action needed to get there.

But what could this action be?

A step in your business?

A change in your life?

A personality transplant?

If you decide NOT to make the changes, if your choice is to NOT move forward, and you decide NOT to take action, then that is your choice and your decision.

BECAUSE NO ONE ELSE IS GOING TO DO THIS FOR YOU.

∞

One of my recent coaches, Cassie, asked me, "_How do you see yourself in the future?_" Knowing my vision in such detail I replied, "_I see myself in my yellow dress, having meetings, in my lovely office, in my five-bed detached house and just living a life of freedom._" She then went on to ask me, "_What are you doing?_" I replied, "_I'm hosting training's, as my dream is to have my own coaching training academy,_" (which in fact, is currently in the formative stages). She then asked: "_What about the coaching you're doing now?_" I replied, "**_Oh, that's all automated._**"

"So, Sam, let me ask you, how much of the future self are you doing now?"

I literally bowed my head in shame and said, **_"Nothing."_** I was so hung up on my desires, that I wasn't acting in alignment to reaching my goals, because I was stuck in the future memory and not being present by doing the things that the future me was doing. This was a clear indication that the action I needed to take now, was as if I am already her - the future me.

Are you doing the things the future version of you is doing?

I can guarantee, you are most probably not. You could potentially be hanging onto the end result and feeling it's never happening and therefore not taking action.

THIS IS WHY IT'S IMPORTANT TO BRING THE FUTURE INTO THE NOW TO CREATE THE LIFE YOU DESIRE.

∞

I was having a breakthrough session with a client the other day, and we went through this exact process of understanding what it was that she really wanted. Once we homed in on her desires, she told me she wanted freedom, success in her business and to move abroad. I then asked her to imagine for a second what it would feel like if her desire was here in the now.

She told me what she saw, what she felt, and what she heard from others as she tapped into the vision using her senses. Sensory acuity is so important when it comes to connecting to your future desires as it enhances your connection to what you really want in the now. Remember, the mind doesn't know the difference between what's right or wrong - it's what feels right for you, so if you constantly think and feel negative things, then that's exactly what you will attract.

Once she opened her eyes, I asked her about what she saw. She told me she saw herself living abroad, celebrating a five-figure month, and feeling utterly grateful and joyous, as if it had already happened.

So, I asked her, *"This future version of you, the actions she's taking, and how she is, can you resonate with any of it? And are you doing any of the future things now?"*

She replied **"No."**

HOW CAN YOU HAVE A VISION DOING THE THING YOU WANT AND NOT TAKE THE STEPS TOWARDS YOUR DESIRES?

It's not just about thinking of it, hoping it will magically happen; it's about feeling the emotions and doing the things you ought to do whilst being the person you want to be, NOW. We are told that if we create a vision board and get all connected to our goals *we will receive* because we are seeing our desires over and over reminding ourselves of what we want. Yes, I do agree in some sense. I mean, I see about ten Porsche turbos every day, so I know my dream car is coming! But it's the constant NEED for the desires, that pushes our ability to achieve it in the now because we are not taking the actions towards achieving it.

When you take ownership for where you are now and start doing more of the things to help you get to where you WANT to be, you instantly feel a shift in your day-to-day actions. It's about doing the things you love without force or expectation and embracing the new you. It's truly magnificent when you start to bring fun into your life as you see the bigger picture of what you truly want, AS YOU OWN YOUR GODDAMN SELF!

∞

VISUALISE AND EMOTIONALISE

What is the worst that can happen if you do something new to better yourself?

The moment we try something new, we instantly feel fear in reaching our fullest potential because of the stories we tell ourselves created in our subconscious mind. Instead of connecting to our visions, we struggle because we feel that it will never happen and just imagine it will all go wrong.

As soon as we feel the fear our nervous system triggers off an emotional reaction causing us to behave and respond to how we really feel, as opposed to how we want to feel. We become numb to change and remain where we are, which is why I feel that most people create addictive traits such as alcohol or drugs, just like I did, to bypass human experiences – our feelings – and avoid any confrontation of the truth that the reality we want isn't here.

We naturally try to protect ourselves and we stop doing the little things to make the world a better place, setting our dreams aside because we have allowed the negative voices in our head to get the better of us.

Don't let the negative stories in your head tell you the way you should live. Embrace the fear and do the things you want to do with love and joy, instead of allowing yourself to become lost and confused. This is why it's so important to emotionally and visually step into our future selves, to become the visionaries and believe that, regardless of what other people's views and thoughts are, we can achieve true success. You can create real change by breaking out of your old belief system.

You are not controlled by your past, it's currently controlling you, and when you acknowledge it and let go of the dead weight, all things become possible because you take back your power. It's about doing the things you want to do, not what is expected or people pleasing or even trying to fit in. It's about what's right for you.

So, take this time to connect to your future self. Bring her into the now, feel the feelings and allow those to take over you. Instead of thinking what if it doesn't work, think *what if it does.*

∞

WHAT YOU CAN HAVE, BE & DO, OPPOSED TO WHAT YOU HAVEN'T, CAN'T & WON'T

We as humans, tend to hang on for dear life to the things we cannot do rather than the things we can but imagine what could happen if instead of focusing on what you can't do, you focus more on what you can.

When I was speaking with my client about her dreams to live abroad and to be a success, I asked her where she was now in relation to her desires. She said, *"I HAVE NOTHING."* Silently shocked at her response because I knew exactly what she has got, I asked, *"So you have absolutely nothing leading you to your desires?"*

She replied, *"Well, I do have 187 team members, **but they're not ALL active**. I do have six figures, **but I'm scared it's going to run out**. I am abroad on holiday, **but we have to go home soon**."*

This client focused more on what she hasn't got than what she has.

HOW ARE YOU EVER GOING TO MOVE FORWARD IF YOU KEEP SEEING THE NEGATIVE IN ALL YOU DO?

This is why it's important to accept, acknowledge and appreciate all the good in your life because believe you me, if you don't, your goals will be pushed further and further away and you're just going to drive yourself crazy. It's about doing the things you want to do, not what you ought to do, by being the person you want to be, opposed to who you don't.

I was hell bent on doing things the way that everyone had told me to do because I thought that's what I had to do. Instead of enjoying the journey, I just despised my work even more because it just didn't feel right.

It's OK to not want to do things that you don't feel obliged to do, especially in your business. Just because others are doing it and it doesn't feel right for you why should you have to do it? This is why I feel it's so important to do the things you love with the belief you can, once you determine all the things you don't like to do. It's OK to be honest because it's essentially your life, *isn't it?*

All that you desire is available for you now. It already exists. It's about seeing the unseen deeply because the power is within you to co-create the life you want, based on your terms, your way. This is why it's vital to switch the conscious awareness into unconscious empowerment and flick that power on by connecting your future into the now.

∞

Δ JOURNAL PROMPT Δ

**It's time to grab your journals and become clear about
what it is that you do want.**

- *What do you no longer want in your life anymore?*
- *What is it you do want, in your life now?*
- *Who are you in the future? What do you look like?*
- *What does your vision of the future look like, feel like and sound like?*
- *What are other people telling you?*
- *What's your self-talk like?*
- *Where are you living and with whom?*
- *How do you feel about everything in your life?*

**Once you have written it all down, close your eyes, and
just imagine yourself in the future. Feel it, see it and
hear the sounds that you know you will achieve whatever
it is you want.**

Once you open your eyes, reflect deeper.

- *What are the things you do in the future, and do you do it now?*
- *If not, what can you bring into the now, and how will you do it?*

When you change your energy, mind and thoughts, then you can truly change your life.

COMMITMENT TO CHANGE

I, _____ solemnly declare that I will acknowledge who I truly am in the future, and I am ready to bring into the now all my desires. I will commit to shifting my perception and change my reality by accepting my past and surrendering to my dreams.

I commit that no matter how hard things will feel, I will be decisive in action, clear in thought, and understand my feelings to the core.

I accept who I am now, and I am ready to bring the future me into the now.

Sign_____Date _____

LEAD WITH DIRECTION, WITHOUT CONFUSION

∞

RELEASE THE PRESSURE

Letting go of the outcome is literally trusting that what you see, is possible for you as you work with intent towards your desires. Intention is very powerful because you trust yourself in your ability to achieve your goals. When you have dreams, desires, and goals, watching the world succeed while yours feels like a million miles away, it can be difficult to imagine it ever happening for you. But all you have to do is:

Let go of the outcome! But how freaking hard does THAT feel?

All my life, I have always been in debt from borrowing in excess to what I could actually earn or receive. The peer pressure from society was well and truly overtaking my life and my need to fit in was at an all-time high. At the prime age of twenty-three, I had accrued over £40k in debt with £20k of it being interest. I was so mad at myself for putting myself in this position and not being able to see a way out, I decided to take out an IVA.

By the time I reached my 30th birthday, I decided enough was enough and declared myself bankrupt. I finally found a job, after a year of no employment and, I finally found my dream man, after years of broken relationships. It was as if I could finally start afresh.

New man, new life. NEW ME.

For several years I was brilliant with my money purely because I had no choice - I wasn't allowed any credit! However, I did learn how to be myself, how to be a mother and of course a wife. These were valuable lessons I had to learn and grow through before I discovered coaching and also when credit came back into my life.

I knew that investment would be key to being better.

Instead of being wise with my spending, I threw every penny I could into my personal development because I hungered for success so badly and I was seeking the right person to help me achieve it.

After making many poor decisions with my investments, and accruing more debt three years into my business, I launched my very first group programme, Unlock Your Money Block®, after successfully having the biggest launch in history.

I had generated £28k in sales for my one-on-one service within six weeks.

I finally had money! I finally got paid! I could finally clear any money I owed!

I decided to close my diary in August 2020 and I invested over £10k into this launch, because if it worked for others, IT HAD TO WORK FOR ME! Instead of being wise with my decisions and looking at a long-term plan, I became obsessed with the outcome and with the thought pondering in my mind, *if you want to make money you gotta spend money,* I threw all the money I could into my launch. I really thought I could make it back quickly, but my fears took over my body as I had never experienced having earned this amount of income before.

I had this awful feeling though my entire being, and I thought,

'WHAT IF I DON'T GET IT AGAIN.'

I had no idea how much this would affect me and began another journey of transition.

With ten days to go until the doors closed to this programme, the panic took over my entire body as not many people had enrolled. I was fearful, emotional and frantically doubting myself to my very core because I wasn't achieving the results I desperately wanted. I set myself up for fifty people to enrol and expected it to happen like everyone else. After all, I did just fill up my one-on-one diary, *right?*

At the time, I wasn't fully aware of how to turn a one-on-one programme into a group programme. I thought it would be no different. But with eighteen one-on-one clients, a group programme underway and another programme launching on the way, I was exhausted with worry and stress because I wasn't clear on my plan. I was clearly NOT ready for a big launch because I was only ever used to one-on-one service and the difference between the two is huge. I became deeply hung up in anticipation of filling the fifty spots and only fifty!

**I couldn't let go of the outcome and I began to wallow
yet again.**

Thankfully, three women did enrol and I was so happy. But the
pure pressure I put on myself made me very poorly and was a
clear indication that I was not ready.

It was not the right time because I was misaligned.

Instead of trusting and believing in myself, I panicked and began
to hire more coaches, completely out of alignment, and paid for a
total of twenty-one programmes in six months. My desperation to
be fixed and chasing the solution left me burnt out and exhausted
and I did not like this feeling at all, and I felt even more confused.

I realised that the constant chasing and my need for success was
blocking my ability to achieve more of what I wanted as I had no
faith in being present in the moment. It was at this point I
realised I had another limited belief causing me to lack trust in
myself.

**I believed I was broken and needed fixing, and that I
was nothing.**

Once I removed these limiting beliefs, things did begin to instantly
shift. My alignment, although uncomfortable, was finally falling
into place as I learned how to trust myself and my decisions. I
took the pressure off myself and deeply surrendered the outcome
because this isn't supposed to be the end, it's the next step to your
next big adventure.

*You gotta be happy with where you are right now, which
means loving mistakes, learning, and moving forward
with joy and gratitude.*

Happiness is a choice. Remember that. And if you don't appreciate where you are now, then the outcome you desire will keep getting pushed further and further away.

You have to trust the person you are about to become - **NOW**.

∞

LIKE FOR LIKE, ALWAYS

For you to have more of what you want, you must first understand what your current beliefs, feelings, and behaviours are before you switch them to ones you do want. It's about trusting that your message is heard, and that you will achieve it simply by letting go of the outcome.

Every time a client invested with me, something wonderful would always manifest into their life. At first, I couldn't believe it. I didn't even see it. When I noticed it, and the more I mastered it myself by letting go of my blocks that caused me to feel stuck and in resistance, the clients would then start to achieve their goals faster!

It could be the perfect job, the love of their life, a marriage, a windfall of income, super strong health and even surgery, simply because they took the pressure off themselves, became aligned to their desired beliefs, and trusted that anything they wanted was possible.

Now, I'm no magical fairy godmother. I want you to have it all, but I cannot do it for you. If you are attracting more of the things you don't want, it's not doing it on purpose. It's happening because your inner world is sending out messages of lack, disbelief, and uncertainty.

This goes the same for people. If like attracts like, yet you are worrying that other people are going to judge you for what you do, then what will happen is that you are going to attract and calibrate the exact way you feel inside, in your outside world. And then what happens? YOU GOT IT! You continue the cycle of self-sabotage.

For example, if you look at how desperately I wanted fifty people on my programme, my sheer desperation was sending out messages that I didn't trust that I would receive. I really do believe if you ask you do receive and if it doesn't come instantly, it's because you are not ready – just like how I was not prepared for a massive group launch.

This is why I say, *I got you, till you got you*, so I can help you hold that space, until you are ready to own yourself.

CAN YOU SEE HOW IT ALL WORKS NOW?

This is how powerful you really are and why you can seriously become a magnet to achieve more of what you want when you reprogramme your subconscious mind.

∞

ALIGN, DECIDE AND BELIEVE

I hope you have already begun to put the pieces of the puzzle together and realise just how incredible these tools are that I am sharing with you. To live your dream life, you need to break down the barriers that prevent you from achieving whatever it is that you want. I know it feels better to blame something, including your past, seeking something to confirm that you will fail, but if you are constantly waiting for everything to fall into place, you will be constantly waiting.

We think that once we learn it all, have it all, look the part, we will succeed, but the only way to succeed is to feel it! You need to feel it now.

How can you achieve your goal if you don't believe it now?

Actions are what will help you to push through and have those major breakthroughs as you begin to take the steps towards making your dream into a reality. Yes, you will make mistakes. Yes, there will be hard times - times of pain, where you want to give up - *like me last week as I close in on completion of this book* - but if you seek perfection over progress, you will continue to meet hardship instead of flowing with ease. I know it sounds quite harsh but it's the truth. I am telling you this because you need to know that failure is a misconception of what you are actually going through.

These are simply lessons of life to help you be YOU!

Everything can fall into place when you become consistent in your actions. You are able to trust your mindset and face challenges head on, shifting from *"why me"* to *"try me"*.

Instead of waiting for the right moment, align, decide and believe in the now, without the worry of tomorrow - it's not here YET. Greet any lessons with open arms and no matter what you go through, keep moving forward at a pace that feels right for you because you will consistently evolve over time to the future version of you as she becomes closer and closer into the present.

∞

THE IMPORTANCE OF VALUES

One of the biggest factors that allows us, as humans, to make decisions aligned to our beliefs are values. Values are basically what is most important to you and supports your ability to make trusted and grounded decisions, backed by deep core beliefs that you can and will achieve whatever it is you desire.

When I help clients align their core values it's either money, business, relationships, health, or spirituality. When I aligned my own values, I chose money. I was so obsessed with it, like an ex-girl-friend unable to let go of a man! (*I say this freely because this was also a very annoying habit I had!*)

It took me forever to get my values into alignment as I never really knew what was most important to me when it comes to money. I lacked faith and trust in my earning potential, and my ability to be a powerful coach, because I had such a horrible relationship with money caused by my poor decision-making abilities and inability to make sound investment choices. I would overspend like I had the money to spare. But I DIDN'T! I was in debt.

My most important value is actually security because it means so much to me. I used to worry about money all the time because I just wanted to make sure that my family is always taken care of. Despite recognising that I had so much love and support from my husband, instead of focusing on my plan A, building a coaching business, I would spend time looking for a part time job to ensure that I would be safe – just like I did when I was in network marketing. But being an entrepreneur is about taking risks, learning to fail with the belief that IT WILL ALL WORK OUT and knowing that there are people around you who do support you.

My fear of not achieving the results fast really hurt me and I would spend days crying when I didn't achieve my goals, as I felt like such a failure. I was seeking a backup plan because I was unable to listen to my needs or pay attention to what I had to do. I lacked patience and trust within myself so I kept seeking another solution, because deep down, I didn't believe success would happen.

But why rush? Why seek? Why not trust and believe?

Throughout my lessons in life, I now believe that there is no plan B - just plan A. Thinking of a backup plan for longer than ten minutes sabotages your plan A and will only prolong your ability to achieve your desires faster, **because you are seeking another solution** rather than focusing on the one you deeply want.

The question bodes, do you even believe you are good enough to achieve a PLAN A?

Feeling the need for a back-up plan will send mixed signals of what you really want causing you to feel even more confused. Yes, you do feel confusion when you are shifting from the old way of thinking, but it doesn't mean you have to confuse your idea. It's important to learn how to be comfortable being uncomfortable, when you are flowing through a transition.

It wasn't until one day when I was telling my wonderful human design mentor, Nina, how I was feeling. She told me:

"SAM, alignment isn't supposed to be easy; it's uncomfortable!"

Getting COMFORTABLE being UNCOMFORTABLE is about knowing how to hold yourself when aligning to your decisions. It's about releasing the old, by feeling the old. It's about becoming the person, aligning to your values and trusting yourself deeply that it will happen!

If you see others achieving success, then please do know, it's going to happen for you too! Just like it has for me when I finally embodied myself for who I am and what I can achieve, by trusting the decisions I made aligning to my core values - especially with money as I became debt free.

That's the true power of value alignment.

∞

VALUE ALIGNMENT

I was mind blown when I discovered how to align your values and it's helped so many people achieve wonderful things. It's so powerful, as you instantly begin to broadcast a strong message through your nervous system and to your subconscious mind, that you are ready. You learn how to trust your ability to make decisions, just like the client I mentioned earlier in the introduction who met the love of her life.

If we don't achieve the results we want, or appreciate what we do have, it's a clear indication that not only are we not in alignment to our values, but also we simply don't believe that we can. The intention is there, which means to *have a plan or/and a purpose to do something with intent.* But if your beliefs and feelings are totally opposite to the intention, you will continue to feel out of alignment thus affecting your ability to make empowered decisions.

I used to see posts on social media all the time stating, **"Oh, I'm back in alignment! I'm feeling myself again!"** I used to think, **God, how do you do that?**

How do you get yourself back into alignment and what does it even feel like?

Being in alignment is literally a connection with heart, mind and spirit where you can make trusted decisions with bat shit crazy faith. You just flow when it comes to being decisive in action without the pressure, whereas being out of alignment feels like there are two parts inside of you – a part in desire of what you want and a part that doesn't feel as if you can achieve it. This then causes us to feel confused and uncertain in our capabilities to achieve our goals because we feel as if all we ever do is make mistakes, and nothing we do is good enough.

***It doesn't matter what action you take if you don't
believe it; your thoughts will always be the victor.***

The lack of clarity and the inability to focus on *what needs to be done*
to achieve your goals, creates a disconnection from what you really
want. Most people are unable to feel what they desire because
consciously, you know what you want, but unconsciously you
don't. This is a clear indication that the choice you made is
misaligned and you begin to send out mixed signals.

*How many times have you thought about something i.e. reaching the next level
in your business because you wanted it so much, but deep down in your heart
you felt that it wouldn't happen?*

You could have the intention that you are going to be persistent
and dedicated in taking action within your business to achieve
your next level of success, or perhaps be a better mum and stop
shouting at the children *(don't worry, we have all been there!)* But no
matter how much you TRY to act with intent based on your decision, you do the complete opposite.

**You make excuses, you procrastinate, and you continue
shouting!**

This is why we sometimes feel stuck with our old habits, because
of the inability to tap inwards. Trapped negative emotions in the
human body connected to some significant event in the past is the
main cause as to why you cannot make decisions aligned to what
really feels right for you; therefore, you project what you really feel
by reflecting it in everything in your outer world feeling as if all
you do is attract crap!

When you start to align to your core values, you make better decisions, and you instantly start to change the way you do things in
your life. You begin to focus more on who you are now and what

you do have, and instantly begin to take back control of your unconscious beliefs, patterns, and behaviours. Instead of *trying* you start *doing* more of what you want because you trust you.

 "Do or do not, there is no try."

— *MASTER YODA*

So be more Yoda, and less Darth Vader. Be in control of you.

Δ JOURNAL PROMPT Δ

Grab your journal, baby; it's time to align your values using this four-step process.

STEP 1

Trust your inner guide to lead you to which area you would like to focus on first.

- *Health /Fitness.*
- *Personal Development.*
- *Relationships.*
- *Family.*
- *Business/career.*
- *Money/Finances.*
- *Spirituality.*

STEP 2

- *Once you select the one you want to work on first, ask yourself:* ***"what is the most important thing to me about that?"*** *Write down as many things as you can. Remember, there is no wrong or right answer. JUST WHAT IS TRUE FOR YOU.*
- *Secondly, let's say for example you selected money,* ***I want you to remember a time when you felt so excited****, before you received money, had money, or just money related. As you remember that specific time,* **what were the feelings you felt at that time?** *Add them to the list of your values.*

STEP 3

Read through the list and if you have repeated anything, if some words could be tweaked, or modified, then do that. Also check for any negations and reframe them to more positive ones that will support you towards your goals, rather than take you away from them.

- *Select your top ten values and ask yourself,* **is no.1 the most important?** *Write down what is so important to you about that and write it in present tense.*
- *Do the remaining values support the top one and do they all align and flow in order that feels right for you?*

∞

This could take you some time, but believe you me, once you align them, you will then be able to look at the list, before you make any decision, such as money, and be able to ask yourself:

"DOES THIS ALIGN WITH MY VALUES?"

If it doesn't, it's not the right decision for you.

If it does, congratulations! You are now able to make trusted decisions based on your values that are true for you.

∞

Place your hand on your heart and say,

"I trust myself, I can be me, and I can achieve whatever I want, because I believe I can."

MIND YOUR TONGUE

∞

BE KIND

As humans, we have a natural tendency to moan if we are not happy with something or someone in our lives. I know things happen, and things can feel uncomfortable, but if you ever knew how powerful your mouth is, you would seriously think again.

In this very existence, especially online, we are living in a connected world but completely disconnected from real people. Cyber bullies and harassment are at an all-time high simply because someone looks a particular way or acts in a particular way or even if they have a different view or opinion.

No wonder we worry so much about other people's opinions!

Instead of focusing on what you can do, as opposed to what you can't, people spend their lives interfering into other people's businesses and feel the need to give their opinion without the consideration of the other person's state, especially if it's something they may not agree with. This not only takes your mind off yourself, but it's actually a confirmation of how much your problem **IS a problem**, because instead of focusing on you, you focus on something else.

Moaning and whinging about yourself only adds more fuel to the fire and the only person you're affecting, is yourself. It will continue to confirm that YES, you are suffering, and prevent you from changing because no one else is.

Let me tell you now, darling, you have got to avoid the moaning.

It's ok to talk to people, but bitching about a problem won't solve it. It's about acknowledging yourself, your issues and your problems FIRST before anything is to ever change whilst protecting your space and energy with clear boundaries.

Judgement without judgement is literally being able to judge other people's opinions or choices without having to judge them for their decision, even if it's against your own.

There are a lot of people in this world who see things differently to how I see the world, to how I feel about things, and I respect them for it. It's not up to me what others decide to do. I accept them for who they are. More and more people are losing the ability to listen or accept another person's choices, thoughts or beliefs and decreasing their ability to improve their EQ because they lack empathy, understanding and connection.

Language and words - *both spoken and thought* - contribute massively towards your ability to achieve what you want. If you lack patience, feel frustrated and make excuses to not take action to achieve whatever it is you want, then how on earth will you ever achieve things faster - AT QUANTUM SPEED - if all you do is spend your time complaining about shit on the telly?

If you don't like someone, **that's ok. Let them be!** If someone has something to say about you, **that's ok. Let them be**. You're only burning your spark out by handing your power over to someone else.

This was one of the biggest and hardest things I ever had to do by keeping myself out of other people's drama, chaos and problems and I think the real reason as to why I became a coach. This is why I say,

"I don't do problems, I DO SOLUTIONS."

If someone does react in a certain way, understand it's not your fault, nor your problem, but have an empathetic understanding of how to communicate effectively to yourself and to others, without coming across as bossy and domineering and worrying about what other people think. As I have said before, PEOPLE ARE NOT THEIR BEHAVIOURS, so quit giving your power to someone else.

∞

OWN YOUR VOICE

Not only must you master your thoughts and your feelings, once you start to stay away from other people's drama and become mindful of your tongue, but you have also got to learn how to master your self-talk.

I have a client who would always first speak in the negative rather than the positive. As much as I love hearing her transition through this process, her conditioning was overruling her ability to master her ability to speak positively about herself because her habit was to speak more negatively.

Most of the women I work with come to me feeling stuck but know giving up is not an option. Yet their language, self-talk and the words they use about themselves and life, are always negative. They desire significant change, results, and create an impact, purely because they know they can. But despite knowing what is possible, they are stuck in the land of *what if it doesn't work,* causing a repetitive strain on their lives, their minds, and on their businesses, purely because their self-talk is always negative.

Life is supposed to be easy, and we are supposed to flow with ease, and joy, which is why your language and words also require reprogramming to be more of what you would like to hear.

I want you to imagine someone you love deeply.

Someone you care about so much. Now imagine, talking to them the negative way you could potentially be talking to yourself.

Will you tell them they are rubbish, call them lazy, or that they can't do it? Would you tell them that they are not good enough and not worthy enough of being successful?

OF COURSE NOT.

Although the transition is required from negative to positive, if you don't talk like this to others, *then why on earth are you disrespecting yourself?*

YOUR PAST CONDITIONING, THAT'S WHY.

I know that you most probably will never give up, because you wouldn't even be questioning yourself, or feeling like this if you weren't on the right path. The path is long and narrow for a reason; to keep you on track. To question oneself is literally shifting from off track to back on track.

Instead of speaking negatively, why not seriously unleash the manifesting mouth from within and bring into fruition what you really want, over what you don't want? When you understand yourself, and master your self-talk too, you begin to heighten your sense of self-awareness, by learning how to regulate yourself and how you are around others. Our self-talk is so vital, both internally and externally because if you use negations in the context of desires, manifestation and affirmations, you will only reject what you really want and block your ability to manifest.

∞

POWER OF WORDS

As I wrote this chapter, I got kind of distracted, and had a look at Facebook. *I do it too, you know!* I noticed a post in a life coaching group and a coach mentioned some affirmations about money that had helped her. She asked which one we (the members) preferred the most. I had a read of them, and I was like, *"NONE."* *I don't think she appreciated my perspective, but I really didn't.*

For example, she mentioned something on the lines of *"Why not me, and why not now?"*

Now, most people will think YES this is PERFECT! But I don't understand HOW? Let me explain this a little more, so you understand why it's vital to master your words both written and spoken. Let's say for example, you ask yourself:

"WHY does life feel so hard?"

The term WHY has a natural tendency to trigger your subconscious mind to reveal to you all the excuses as to why you can't, as opposed to why you can, because you already know why you can't. Your subconscious programming (self-limiting beliefs and experiences from your past) wants to confirm to you that YOU

ARE RIGHT because life has most probably felt hard as you start to remember memories, feelings and connections to events where it did. So, if you say, *why not me*, then imagine all you are going to think and feel are reasons as to why it can't be you.

Can you see my point?

This is why affirmations don't always help or work when you have a negative mindset because you don't deeply believe in yourself. Look I get it! Everyone talks about affirmations, and I DID IT TOO! I Looked in the mirror every day, talking to myself like a fucking lunatic, smiling at myself, and it does work - but it only works for short term gain, instead of helping you achieve long term results.

Affirmations do work, WHEN you remove the old beliefs, thoughts and feelings as you make room for new beliefs, thoughts and feelings.

However, you still have to learn how to transition from a negative to positive. So instead of saying LIFE IS HARD or LIFE IS EASY, what you could say is,

I know life feels hard at the minute, but I know I am on my way to an easier life.

I know things feel challenging right now, but I know

I am on the right path to my desires, and anything is possible.

Can you see what I did there?

Can you see how the transition from your current state to desired state ought to be one of ease and flow?

This is why I recommend the following to help you really own your words and take charge of your manifesting mouth, because believe you me, YOU CAN.

Address the Current Problem

Instead of brushing the problem away, address it and ask yourself - *I'm finding things really hard right now, what can I do to make things easier?* Most people want to ignore the inner critic and avoid confrontation and facing their problems.

When you raise awareness of what is actually happening and how you are currently feeling, you take ownership of where you are now, allowing you to safely accept what the next step is for you as you take the leap of faith with ease, like a baby learning to walk. It's about understanding what you currently believe and how you feel to understand where you are now.

Reframe Your Self Talk

When your subconscious mind has deep integrated limitations, it feels quite challenging to flick any type of sentences from negative to positive ie. *Life is hard* to *life is easy.* This can lead to an increase in anxiety and stress which causes dysfunction within the flow of the human body. Simply by pausing, reflecting, and reframing, you will be able to tap into yourself more and begin to start facing any problems with ease.

Avoid the word STOP

Saying to yourself *I have to stop making things so hard*, or *I have to stop being so hard on myself*, will only push you harder to not stop because you already believe that things are hard. When you shift your perception and inner language to more of what feels right, and true for you, you give yourself permission to pause, breathe and reflect without the need of taking a U-TURN as you become kinder to yourself.

Stay Away from Drama

Honestly, it's not worth it. Just do your best to pull away from it all and let go of the need to be involved. It's not going to pay your bills! Get yourself an elastic band, put it on your wrist and keep pulling it back and letting it go, as you pull yourself back from the need of interfering and voicing more negativity.

LIFE GETS TO BE EASY WITH YOU IN THE DRIVER SEAT.

The power is within you, tap into it.

∞

LANGUAGE IS NOT ALWAYS THE BARRIER

You may be thinking, hang on? You just told me to mind my tongue?

YES, I did, but did you also know that your body talks too?

As much as your self-talk and how you communicate to others is vital and important to having a mastered mind, it's also about being an empathic listener. It's not just about hearing words, it's about feeling other people's feelings too as there is a lot of nonverbal communication hidden in the body.

To be able to read another person's body language is another skill that can be learned and linked very much to empathy. When you can understand the postures, expressions and even their eye movements, you can not only begin to decode their behaviour, but also begin to understand what it is that they are really thinking and feeling and what could have potentially caused them to feel the way they do.

When I pick up on a client's body language, it allows me to intuitively ask questions that allows them to think deeper and begin to shift from effect to cause as they change their perspective. This creates a greater impact in their session with a bigger breakthrough and release process as they begin to understand themselves at a whole new level.

For example, a client enrolled into my one-on-one programme in January 2021 because she wanted to create her own business and feared that she couldn't do it as she felt she was always second best in everything she did. She cancelled her initial calls for the first month as she became very poorly and was soon after diagnosed with a stomach problem and advised that she would need major surgery. Obviously, the client was super upset as she really wanted to begin her inner work first. Little did she know that her body was purging by bringing the negativity to the surface, simply because she decided she had enough of being second best and wanted to change.

We began her one-on-one programme in March, two months later, and by the second session, she couldn't stop herself from crying as her fear of going to hospital was causing major discomfort.

By tapping into the client's needs, I realised that her body was taking over her ability to speak, and I applied my energy healing method, silent counselling, to ease the sabotage from her body. This is such a powerful modality that allows you to release the negative emotions from your physical body using your meridians as we do hold onto a lot of negative energy throughout our human vehicles. Within forty five minutes, the client was calm and peaceful and was blown away that she no longer felt so emotional.

By week three, she had a call from the doctor and received a second opinion. She was advised that she could, in fact, heal naturally. Super excited to hear this, we continued to work deeper and released the negative emotions stored in her subconscious mind around her health using Time Line Therapy®.

By week six she went back to the doctors and they told her that **she had healed**. She wouldn't need surgery and they were amazed at what had happened.

OMG. Even I was blown away!

By understanding the human body and how this client felt, I was able to tap into what she needed and heal at a subconscious level as 95% of our responses are determined by our subconscious mind. If this is the case, and you have so many negative blocks, then how can anyone ever survive with just 5% of positive intentions? No wonder everything feels so hard!

This is exactly why affirmations are challenging at first, when 95% of you believes, feels and projects that everything is hard.

With the mind-body connection so strong and powerful, it is important to understand how you feel, why you feel it and how it affects your own physiology and physicality. When you are able to understand another person, this again will allow you to create stronger relationships with others, because you are aware of yourself, with the ability to empathise with others, and therefore create better and improved relationships.

Another great reason why it's important to increase emotional intelligence.

∞

Δ JOURNAL PROMPT Δ

Grab your journals; it's time to speak the hell up!

YOU:

- *What is your current self-talk like?*
- *What are all the negative things that you tell yourself?*
- *Do you tend to start conversations speaking in negations? If so, how can you now start to shift from negative to positive?*
- *What affirmations do you tell yourself that you feel don't work?*
- *What affirmations do you want to believe?*
- *Write down 100 things you love about yourself and your life and do it with intention!*
- OTHERS:
- *Be really honest, are you an XOXO gossip queen?*
- *Why do you feel the need to gossip, and what do you really get out of it? BE HONEST.*
- *What negative things have you said about other people either to them or behind their backs?*
- *Now that you have spoken your truth, how do you feel about gossiping, and what will you do now to prevent yourself from inviting other people's chaos into your life?*
- *Write a forgiveness letter to yourself and to others.*

Place your hand on your heart, close your eyes and say out loud:

"I forgive myself. I forgive others. It's safe to speak kindly about myself and others.

I give myself permission to be free from the negativity and just be."

I highly recommend Louise Hay's book "Heal Your Body" as it really does make sense as to why your body feels the way it does and how you can heal from within.

THE POWER REALLY IS WITHIN YOU!

YOUR OUTER WORLD IS YOUR INNER WORLD

∞

The only person responsible for change is you. No one else is going to make you do it.

As the ex-PRO in procrastination, I had some serious issues with getting organised. I would leave things to the last minute, snap and blame everyone for being late because it's not my fault, *is it?* This caused more chaos in the outside world and I was left feeling extremely frustrated in the inside world for not getting anything done on time.

When I first began to work with a coach in 2017, she would give me weekly tasks to complete. I would be so excited to complete them, but as soon as an hour would pass, I would pause, take a break, and the next thing you know, a week had passed and I'd have done nada! She would ask me how I got on and I would reply, *"Yeah, I'm getting there!"* But deep down I was petrified because I knew I was leaving it to the last minute and I knew I wasn't going to complete my work.

I had this tendency to STOP AND START EVERYTHING AND ANYTHING.

Most people tend to say to get over procrastination, all you need to do is *make a list, get organised, become self-disciplined, just get on with it* and *get out of your own way*... blah blah blah! As much as this sounds doable, it's a lot easier said than done, *right*? YES! They eventually WILL help, but first you need to understand where this behaviour stems from so that you can move forward with ease.

HOW CAN YOU SEE CLEARLY IN THE DIRECTION YOU NEED TO GO, IF YOU CAN'T MOVE FORWARD? FURTHERMORE, WHAT IS IT THAT'S REALLY HOLDING YOU BACK?

I would never complete courses, constantly make excuses such as *the kids distracted me, the housework took over*, and my favourite *I was tired*. I wasn't taking responsibility for my actions because I wasn't shown how to or even knew how to. Instead, I just worried about money, with a deep feeling of guilt putting more pressure on my body, creating time limits and great stress to my immune system. When we apply pressure, we physically and mentally cannot focus on a thing nor do more than one thing at a time because we are emotionally exhausted. This is why the real core reason behind procrastination is not about productivity, it's about EMOTIONS.

∞

DECLUTTER THE CHAOS

In 2014, we moved into a three-floor flat, a converted loft in an old Victorian house. The first floor was our bedroom, the second floor was where the boy's room, the kitchen and the children's playroom was based, and the top floor was the living and dining area.

In 2016, we had just returned from a very stressful holiday in Cyprus as both myself and my eldest caught Hand, Foot and Mouth disease. Ewww! It was gross. I couldn't eat! My mouth was full of ulcers and it felt like I had the flu. After a week had passed from our return, feeling chilled, relaxed and ready to take on the world, I remember sitting on the top floor and I felt this bug on my arm. I instantly felt itchy, *(if you are itching now, my apologies! I'm ITCHING TOO!)* and decided to blitz and bleach the entire room.

I sat down again at the end of the day, and felt another bug; in fact there were three. I freaked out, because in our previous flat back in 2013, *one week before I gave birth to my youngest,* the flat had a flea nest that just emerged from the ground and broke out and created a home in my sofa. *I had the entire flat fumigated and was not happy!* So when these little bugs emerged from the sofa in 2016, I was having serious flashbacks and was instantly triggered!

Just before our holiday to Cyprus my mum who came with us had said to me, *"Sam, you have some bugs in the boy's rooms. Be sure to clean it down!"* I was like, *"YES MUM!"* (You know what mums are like). With this thought in my mind, I went into the boy's room and I saw that there were more little bugs all over the window sill.

I instantly went onto Google to search for this bug and discovered that they were carpet beetles. However, these were not the bugs in the living room. I thought to myself right, *we got bugs in the boy's room, and bugs on the sofa that are not the same. ARE THEY FLEAS?* I instantly went into panic and analytical mode and began to think of what could have been brought up to the top floor.

My eldest had brought up a book from their playroom the night before, so I went down to the second floor and I looked at the book rack. As I looked closely, I noticed that the entire wall was infested with BUGS - the smallest little bugs you could imagine as if there were pencil dots all over the wall. It was all over the toys, the books, EVERYWHERE!

I CRIED.

Behind the book rack was a door to the rooftop and in there, was a nest of pigeons that I had refused to handle. The pigeons had passed through pigeon fleas, carpet beetles, **the works and** infested my entire house. This was by far the most stressful moment of my life and I couldn't stop crying.

I then had this urge to remove the clutter from underneath the boy's beds. As I did, I discovered something quite disgusting. A MASSIVE NEST FULL OF SKIN SHELLS & MORE BUGS!

How could I have allowed myself to live and create a life like this AROUND MY CHILDREN!

The bugs had manifested everywhere - the bathroom, kitchen cupboards, the beds, the wardrobes - **MY FUCKING WARDROBE!**

It was at this point I realised how much I had neglected my actual reality by projecting my inner perception of my negative world into my existing world.

I was disorganised. I lacked appreciation. I was a hoarder!

My constant need for money and success and the inability to achieve it, was a clear indication how much I was more focused on the outcome than what I had by ignoring my home and my loved ones. My emotions were at an all-time high and I had enough of feeling this way. I literally screamed out loud,

"FUCK THIS, I AM DONE! Nothing is more important than my family and my home."

I have never felt so disgusted with myself in all my life.

So, the fumigation began and I decluttered everything. I couldn't clean the house for two weeks, but I did eliminate at least fifteen bags of rubbish. The pigeons had to be removed and it took a good eight weeks for me to recover as it made me really poorly. This is why hoarding, mess and clutter, are not good for the mind or for yourself as it really does prevent you from focusing more on the inner world, when the outside world is so chaotic.

It took this crash to seriously realise that I had to get my shit in order if I was ever to become a serious entrepreneur in this world.

Soon after, I began to treat my home a whole lot differently. I would go around cleaning like a mad woman in a complete state of gratitude.

"Thank you for this cloth! Thank you for this hoover. Thank you for my working arms so I can clean!"

When you clear the mind, you clear your world, because your outer world is your representation of who you are. To manifest and achieve your goals, it's vital to understand yourself with clarity and conviction because when you do, you achieve everything you want and more, *without the bugs.*

∞

GET ORGANISED

As much as decluttering the outside world is so important for mental clarity, so is decluttering your inner mind.

I used to LOVE A LIST! My sister told me that I would always write lists upon lists upon lists when I was younger. I personally don't remember it myself, however, I do know that anytime I had a big project, big launch or something to do, I would get it down on a list.

As much as a list helps, it won't if you don't get anything done. One of the greatest things I ever learned in 2016, was from a coach called Niyc Pidgeon who explained this wonderful process called NOW, SOON, LATER. It was my first experience with a coach, and I absolutely loved it. At the time, I was in network marketing, but her energy shifted something for me back then. Perhaps she was sent to me to plant the seed of becoming a coach? Who knows because everything does happen for a reason, hey?

She advised that we should organise our thoughts, actions and things that need to get done into three columns as follows:

1. NOW.

Write down all the things that require urgency. Things that need to get done in the next 24-48 hours.

2 – SOON.

Write down all the things that need to get done in the next week.

3 – LATER

All the other things in order that could be done later in the month, or thereafter.

The purpose is to cross off the now, move later and soon to now, to help you stay on track. By emptying your mind of your chaos, you will instantly begin to feel lighter as you now know all the things that you have to do. *Isn't it such a wonderful way to organise your mind, thoughts and actions?* ***I think so!***

So much so, that it's become a natural habit for me to do so without the need of writing down huge lists. I journal everything down that I need to do and just go with the flow.

I won't take credit for this because it was Niyc that taught me this, so thank you Niyc. It's changed my life as well as my client's.

The next thing I would then advise is to plan out when you will be able to take the actionable steps by getting your time organised. I personally dedicate my working week to do the things I want to do when the children are at school. Find the times that suit best for you and become responsible for the actions that you take by giving yourself the flexibility to shift things around when you feel the need to do so. Get yourself organised, declutter the shit out of your life and take back control of both your inner and outer world.

∞

Fears, doubts, and 'lack of' are just negative things that can be eliminated so THAT YOU CAN start to gain trust in yourself and your journey.

*If there is no faith, there is no belief.
Without belief, then what do you have?*

The more you acknowledge, accept and appreciate, the more strength you will gain in you because you trust you.

The power that exists within you is so infinite that once you unlock it, you will be amazed at how powerful you really are!

∞

PART III
ELIMINATION

Neutralise the past with trust in the future.

The only reason you feel stuck is because you are living in fear of the future, held back by the past. When you let go of the past and gain trust in the present, you become present, in the moment, AS YOU.

What you think you know:

That everything will be fine as long as you work hard.

What you require to know:

That you will keep repeating old habits and feel the same, unless you eliminate the root cause.

What you don't know:

That your subconscious mind actually wants you to release the bullshit, hence why it keeps regurgitating in your life every day. Your body wants to heal.

THE PROCESS

∞

I am sure you can now see and understand that if you keep putting a plaster over the wounds *(aka inner blocks)*, this will continue to prevent you from healing deeply, unless you get to the root of your underlying problems. This is why in this section, I will be discussing exactly why it's important to deeply heal and how when you do, you unlock your potential at a cellular level.

I really do believe from my experience and my clients, that the only true way to eliminate any blocks and limitations from the mind, is via one-on-one coaching. **You just have to be ready.** When you are, my diary is open for you so email me at;

sam@samevansglobal.com for more details. However, in this part, I will explain to you how my process works and why the problems even exist and how they are created.

∞

THE METHOD

As a master coach in very powerful modalities, based on my own experiences with the use of Time Line Therapy®, it's the only method that eliminates the root cause of EVERY self-sabotaging block (thank you, Daniel)! Using this modality, it will take you back unconsciously to the first event known as the Gestalt, which is the significant moment that created a patterned way of thinking, feeling and behaving based on your past experiences.

The women who reached out to me, all came to me with the exact same patterns of behaviour as I did.

- *They had no idea what was wrong but knew something had to be done.*
- *They felt stuck in survival mode, frustrated and fed up.*
- *Anytime they tried to work on themselves, nothing worked.*
- *They were ready to shift!*

Through years of practice and research, I created my own framework using these tools which has now helped hundreds and soon to be thousands of women across the globe. Introducing, The Cognitive Switch® Method.

My four-part framework is as per the following diagram.

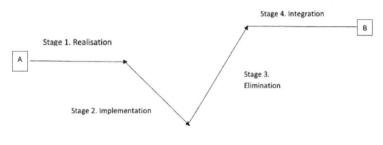

A represents the CURRENT STATE. *This is where you feel comfortable, safe and secure.*

B represents the DESIRED STATE. *This is where you hold your dreams and aspirations of where you want to be.*

See how A is slightly lower than the B?

That's because to reach your next level requires a shift from the old world into the new world by rewiring the beliefs and releasing the negative emotions attached to your past.   In other words, it's about leaving the excess luggage that's weighing you down so you can freely move within your journey of evolution.

If you are unable to break through, no matter how hard you push yourself, you just end up feeling burnt out and even more frustrated, as if you are going one step forward, ten steps back.

You cannot see your blind spots and self-sabotage kicks in. The inner critic barks like a mad dog and the negative emotions surface to the horizon, causing you to feel deflated and basically, you can't be bothered, because nothing you do is ever good enough.

Your model of the world is your internal representation of how you think, feel and act; so when it comes to doing anything new, if you have experienced something negative in the past, then these feelings will keep coming back because you haven't worked through them.   This will then cause your behaviour to act out according to what you unconsciously believe to be true.   This state keeps repeating itself because your past is controlling your every move in the present.

This is why when I begin with a new client, stage one is about **realising** where they are now and what's been holding them back.   I help them see their blind spots and guide them through to stage two where they begin to start **implementing** new ways to take inspired action towards their desired goals. By following this process, the client will instantly begin to see significant changes in their life as things begin to fall into place, exactly how they wanted.

Once a client begins to implement their new ways into the present, their mind begins to trust me and allows me to enter into the subconscious for the releasing process as we *eliminate* the old ways of thinking and feeling by breaking through into the new as they surrender their past.

Now see how implementation drops down?

As soon as the elimination process begins, you will start to purge and release the old thoughts, feelings and behaviours which can feel quite uncomfortable. Once everything settles, your body wants to integrate the new ways, which is stage four. This again takes time and patience with a willingness to surrender the old and unlocking a completely different version of you whilst still being you.

YOU MUST UNLEARN WHAT YOU KNOW, SO THAT YOU CAN LEARN TO EVOLVE.

∞

BREAKDOWN TO BREAKTHROUGH

Whilst the purging and breaking down the old ways feels uncomfortable, it really is a clear sign and indication that you are reaching your next level of wherever you desire to be.

Google defines a breakthrough *as an important discovery or event that helps to improve a situation or provide an answer to a problem.* It's about breaking down the old ways of thinking and breaking through into the new by unlearning, releasing and reframing your past attachments and old habits that are sabotaging you from having success, without having to relive them.

Your natural response to a breakthrough could be tiredness, yawning, confusion, and it can even stir up old negative emotions that you thought you had left well and truly in the past. The only reason why they do come up, is because they have come up to pass. *Kinda like when you feel nauseous and you feel the need to be sick.* Except this time, you actually do throw it all up. Yes. It's not always pretty, hence why *you gotta get comfortable being uncomfortable.*

It can sometimes feel like you are having a breakdown because you are releasing negative emotions, but the lessons you face are here to help you become stronger. Believe it or not, the harder they feel, the more powerful the results will be.

By learning from an event will not only allow you to move forward and become free from the past, but you start to feel freaking incredible in everything that you do.

If it ever feels too uncomfortable then what you can do is ask yourself, *what can I do to help me push through this breakthrough?*

This is the power of letting go and how by taking responsibility will reignite your power to achieve anything you desire.

We will never stop having breakthroughs or face challenges in our lifetime, especially if we want to create anything positive in our lives. This however, will always be down to your choice - do you **BACK UP** or *BREAKTHROUGH?*

THE MIND

∞

EVERYTHING BEGINS IN THE MIND

Despite having a new fresh mentality after realising how much I was avoiding the problem and having to face it *(the realisation)*, and by taking responsibility on how much that I had to take action now by getting my life organised *(implementation)*, my inner world was really purging out my soul and I still had no idea what I had to do in order to be successful *(hello, stage 3 - elimination)*.

When you work for someone else, it's like you're on autopilot. You get up, you go to work, you come home, you go to sleep *and then repeat*. It's only when you become self-employed that you have to learn how to be responsible for yourself by reconditioning your olds ways into the new ways with a solid mindset.

The only person you can ever truly rely on is yourself.

I really did expect that by reading *The Secret*, listening to my positive audios and reciting my affirmations, that all was going to be super-freakin-mazing. I did this for around two years during my network marketing day and all it did was drive me insane! Any time I did NOT listen to the audios, or repeat my affirmations, I would just explode. My husband once said to me,

"SAM, when you don't listen to the audios, you act like a right prick!"

I just laughed it off, but he was right, *with love of course.*

None of this stuff was working because my negativity was so deeply embedded, that any time I tried to apply my mind work, I was actually pushing my problems deeper inside as I was avoiding them at all costs. I had no idea how to let my negativity go and no matter how many coaches, energy healers, and self-study work I applied into my life, nothing was getting to the root of it all, until I became a coach.

I initially began my coaching career as a business coach, helping women create consistent incomes online with automation. I absolutely loved how you could make things easy online and instantly fell in love with the process. However, every time I held a strategy call, the women didn't want to create automated systems; they wanted help with their mindsets. For some strange reason, they kept coming to me and all I kept hearing was this little voice inside of me saying,

"There has got to be another way to help women with their minds."

This was when I met Daniel Tolson in 2018, my incredible mentor who introduced me to the world of NLP and Time Line Therapy®. I Invested in his practitioner course as I thought, *why not! I could learn a few new tricks, I'm a badass, I know my muvva-luvin' LOA!!*

Or so I THOUGHT!

This course was over a duration of five days in Birmingham, where I literally transitioned from this cocky emotional little girl to a grown ass woman. I spent six hours per day, travelling to and back from my course because I was committed to making this change happen. *That, and the fact that Daniel had told me that I had to come or else, because I almost quit before I even started as I tried to cancel going, days before the training began.* **He had already sussed me out and called me out on my bullshit!**

At first, I felt ok. I was listening and making notes, learning through observation and I thought, *mmm this is something that could potentially change a lot of women's lives.* However, by day three I became an emotional wreck. I couldn't stop crying and Daniel could see how much pain I was holding onto and he used an NLP technique called the *New Orleans Drill* that allowed me to cry my last tear.

Please note: this method can only be experienced with a qualified coach, in an offline session, and how I would never offer this service online due to the nature of the work involved. Daniel is a master coach and trainer extremely experienced which is why I'm so grateful he gifted me with this healing process.

After the session I felt absolutely amazing as if a new lease of life had entered into my body. But by day four, I spiralled again as my deep-rooted anger returned to the surface and came bursting out, exactly like it did on day twenty-one of my self-healing with Reiki.

I WAS SO MAD THAT I LOST IT WITH EVERYONE IN THAT ROOM THAT DAY. AND YOU KNOW WHAT, THEY ALL HELD THAT SAFE SPACE FOR ME, AND FOR THAT I CAN'T EVEN BEGIN TO EXPRESS MY GRATITUDE.

It was as if my spirit finally felt safe to let out the pain and hurt because no one else had managed to help before. By surrendering my own self-sabotaging emotions and beliefs, I finally felt for the very first time as if I could breathe deeply and my spirit felt free.

My voice changed. My physiology changed. My behaviour changed. Everyone noticed it.

This journey for me was not just about learning new tools; it was about embodying the power of it all, healing me first and then being able to give it to others.

Despite having such a massive breakthrough, two weeks after completing my course, I started to feel really emotional again, and I couldn't understand why.

How could I feel so messed up again? I thought I was free?

I THOUGHT I WAS HEALED?

I had a lot more layers to remove as I had only scratched the surface with my own subconscious healing which is why I invested in my first NLP coach, Jo, who helped me to connect WITH THE REAL ME.

I feel and believe that you have to work with the right mindset coach who really gets you, and with Jo, she just got me. Every time she held a session, it was really difficult for me to let go of the old ways and I always felt like I'd been hit by a tornado. But she held that safe space for me and for that, I am forever grateful.

Thanks to her patience, guidance and calmness - *and her ability to manage my obsessive crazy million voice notes every day (yes, I was that neurotic)* - she helped me surrender so many of my deep-rooted blocks and beliefs that were trapped in my subconscious mind. She helped me transition into the woman I am today, which has led me to help so many women across the globe achieve the same.

I really do believe that because of the power involved with these techniques and how the process of elimination has helped all of my clients become completely free from their self-sabotaging behaviours, that I have inspired and guided many of my clients to become NLP coaches so that they could pass on the freeness to other people too.

I look at Facebook every day, seeing so many women suffering and hiding behind their masks because they haven't been able to release their bullshit. But I cannot force or help anyone unless they want to help themselves, exactly like how I did. I believe that *when the student is ready the teacher will appear,* just like Daniel and Jo did for me and my third mentor, Ewan Mochrie.

I met him in 2019 when I became a master coach. Again, I approached this training slightly cocky, but *I was like OK! Let's learn a few more tricks!* Little did I know that I was about to release my sexual trauma which was linked to my phobia of heights. I had no idea that this was the case and that I hadn't even released my sexual trauma with Jo. I had released so much with her, that I didn't even think it was still there.

Between the ages of six and seven I was sexually abused by my uncle, my dad's brother who lived in Germany and we used to visit him travelling by ferry. My physical body had already decided that it would not be best to travel to Germany, as unconsciously it would remember what had happened and it was trying to pull me back; the only way it could was to create a phobia.

The first time we went to visit him when I was eight years old, the sea was very rocky with torrential rain and my family decided to go up onto the top deck. They all scurried off in front of me and I was left to wander up the stairs by myself as the ferry rocked horrifically, side to side. Despite it being a very slow ferry, the fear of going upstairs alone, literally took over my body as I was petri-fied, trying to hold onto the sides and begging someone to help me. I didn't realise that this phobia would leave me feeling so nervous and shaken as if my entire world was closing around me, to the point that I couldn't even look out of the window if I ever travelled over bridges over water.

This phobia was the only way that I could protect myself from what happened to me as a child and therefore creating the biggest and toughest barrier I could to never let this ever happen again. Looking back now, I realised that I had to be ready to reach this point of breaking through from the past which thankfully Ewan helped me release and for that again, I am also forever grateful.

We all have a desire to be more, to have more and to learn more. But when we desire to start something new, we begin to suddenly feel overwhelmed with fear and doubt whether the new venture will ever work out. What we actually want to feel is CONFI-DENT, EMPOWERED, MOTIVATED, CONSISTENT, PERSISTENT AND DISCIPLINED; but instead, we are left feeling stuck in the comfort zone and disempowered to take any inspired action.

So how on earth do we create such limitations?

I will now explain in the simplest way possible exactly how.

∞

MIND-BODY CONNECTION

Before birth

From the moment we are conceived, we absorb sounds from outside of the womb and even absorb our mother's emotions and beliefs, and begin to program our subconscious minds. We start banking them without even knowing that we are and begin to create our perception of the outside world from inside the womb.

After birth

As soon as we are born up until the ages of two to three, we begin to learn unconsciously where we do things without even realising before it becomes an unconscious habit. For example, I remember when my youngest had his first treasure basket at five months old, and he picked up two objects and banged them together not realising that he had made a pair. Within a few minutes, he had this look of wonder on his face, as he just realised that he had made a match and had no idea how he did it and continued repeating this behaviour every time he played with his basket. *I love this baby stage of wonder!*

By the time children reach the age of two, things begin to change. Instead of once appearing cute and adorable, children's emotions begin to play a huge impact on how they behave. Most people call the two-year old phase the *terrible twos,* I mean, why would you? It's not as if children want to be terrors? They are just becoming more aware of their emotions based on their experiences and are just learning to express themselves, no matter how annoying it feels.

Children's brainwave cycles between the ages of birth to seven, are in the alpha and theta stages which are relatively slow cycles yet the same ones that adults experience when they are either meditating (aka alpha) and when they go under hypnosis (aka theta).

During the theta stage between the ages of two to six years, children walk around in a constant state of hypnosis absorbing everything up like a sponge. Because they have a higher level of suggestibility and receptivity, they begin to believe everything that is told to them and become more oriented to their inner world than their outer world.

By learning about their world around their family, friends and the wider community, they begin to form their values and their beliefs about themselves based on what feels true to them.

These beliefs stay with the children like scripts which are defined *as a mental representational format.* It outlines the basic actions needed *(which represents how we feel, act and behave to have a sense of belonging and the need to feel safe),* to complete a more complex action *(how we respond to the outside world).* It's these perceptions *(albeit positive or limiting)* that we form, create and trust as we carry these scripts into our adulthood.

Children become more conscious of what they do as they start to make decisions with awareness and curiosity. *Kinda like sticking a screwdriver in a plug socket to see what happens, or putting their hands on the stove, to see if it burns!* **It's not safe and yes it burns!** Although children are egocentric, they do find it difficult to see the viewpoints of others.

Children then begin to make subconscious decisions about how they need to behave or be, just so they can gain approval from their loved ones, which is then reflected later on adulthood. This is why the early years play a crucial role in our overall development because of the conditioning from our environment as we absorb everything around us and we programme our minds. *(Can you see why Montessori was a freaking legend)?*

We as adults naturally feel overly protective of our children and based on our own upbringing, unconsciously, we reflect our past conditioning onto our children and we tell them off, by shouting *"No!"* and *"Don't do that,"* which the child then absorbs during these very impressionable ages. They absorb everything that is heard, everything that is felt and everything that is seen, exactly how we did when we were children. *(Again, there is no judgement here.*

I raised my voice many times when my two were toddlers, because of my own upbringing – I didn't know any different to what I had experienced as a child).

As children we were never taught about the power of the mind or how it will affect us as adults. Our childhoods were stifled by being told what we *should* and *shouldn't do*; to be *good little boys and girls* and if we weren't, we were **naughty** when all we really wanted to do was to have fun and be free.

As adults, we try to replace the old perceptions with new ones, but we find it difficult and confusing because we lack the ability to trust and listen to ourselves, most probably because as children we were *"not listening."* This leads us to feel misaligned from our desires, confusing our very existence and therefore unable to take on responsibility. The once happy and free child becomes trapped in a box and the vicious cycle of generational wounds continues.

No wonder we feel lost, and uncertain!

If we as adults are constantly building a shithouse on a foundation that's gonna crumble because of our past conditioning, then how do we even begin to change the way we think, feel and behave to have, be and do what we really want? We have to go deep in the mind and pluck out the roots that cause us significant pain by nurturing our land to build a new foundation. You have to get to the root of the problem just like you would eliminate the roots of the weeds in the gardens.

In other words,

YOU HAVE TO CHANGE YOUR CURRENT REALITY BY FACING THE PAST.

There will always be something deeply buried within your subconscious mind that will require healing to help you confidently move forward. You can call it healing, you can call it eliminating, you can call it whatever you want, the only way you will ever start rebuilding is if

You release your unconscious feelings (create new foundations).

You rewire your subconscious thoughts from the past (build new walls).

And you reprogramme your subconscious behaviour (have a fresh new door).

You have the power to heal everything, and that power has to come from within you.

PHEW! That's enough mindset jargon from me!

∞

HEALING THE ROOT CAUSE

I see so many women posting on social media about how they suffer with anxiety.

I ask myself, *if you know that you are suffering with it, why are you not addressing it and understanding that there is something that can be done, instead of allowing it to consume your very existence?*

I used to be a massive anxiety sufferer and it was only when I released my attachment to the future by eliminating the root from the past, I was finally able to have trust in everything I did.

Google's definition of anxiety is a *feeling of worry, nervousness, or unease about something with an uncertain outcome.* In fact, according to research, women in the UK were reported to have 24% higher levels of anxiety compared with men, in 2020. So, if your anxiety is caused by feeling worried and uneasy about something in the future, then wouldn't it be energetically better to understand w*hat you are specifically worried about? And how did it become so apparent?*

The inability to shift from current state to desired state prevents us from moving forward and therefore we resist change. This is also known as an inner conflict and what self-sabotage truly is. It's only when you understand where you are now and how you got there, you can shift your entire perception when you eliminate the root cause.

Now you may think that this is easier said than done and you could potentially consciously know this, yet unconsciously, your subconscious will not allow you to understand because it doesn't know how to or want you to change. The unease affects your body and prevents you from moving forward, causing self-sabotage.

The negative thought triggers a negative feeling; this causes negative behaviour which returns negative feedback (aka like for like).

If anxiety is fear of the unknown, then the inner work required is to deeply understand that this fear is caused by over-excessive worry of a future that hasn't even happened yet. The mind doesn't know the difference between what's right or what's wrong, so whatever you think or feel deep down, you will believe it to be true, even if you have no idea why you feel this way.

We are only born with two innate fears: the fear of falling and the fear of loud sounds. All the other fears consumed along our lifetime are based on experiences that we go through. *So, if fear of the future stems from fear of the past, what happened to you in the past that caused you to worry about a future that hasn't even happened yet?*

The excessive worries and fears cause you to live in the present, feeling as if you are stuck with resistance to change because, instead of understanding why you feel this way, you just assume it's just you and that nothing can be done. But every single one of us has the power to be authentic and empowered. Despite this not being or feeling apparent, no matter how much you tell yourself, *you are ok, fine, and it will all blow over,* the problem will keep repeating itself in your outer world, unless you dig deep into the inner world.

Ever wonder why your mind goes into overdrive with thoughts?

Your subconscious mind hasn't fully healed or uncovered your root cause of self-sabotage which then goes around that vicious cycle when really, it wants you to pay attention to it.

So how do you get to the root cause?

Time Line Therapy®. That's how.

∞

EMOTIONAL CONNECTION TO THE PAST

One of my recent clients told me that she was a serial procrastinator and that it was causing her much pain in her life. Every time she attempted to take inspired action, something in her life would happen which would prevent her from moving forward.

She felt as if she never had any time and she would snap and shout at her children because they never gave her the time to do the things she wanted to do. But it's never about the kids - **it's always about us.**

I asked her a set of questions to understand as to why she felt she was procrastinating and how it was affecting her. The more we dug deeper, the more her emotions stirred up; the more she responded, the more uncomfortable she became, as we were reaching closer to understanding why she loved what she was doing even though she didn't want to, which in this case, was procrastinating.

The root cause of her behaviour as to WHY she was procrastinating had nothing to do with time or anything to do with her children.

She believed that she was going to die at 46.

Now you could be thinking, **WHAT!?** *How on earth IS THIS the reason as to why she procrastinated?*

Her unconscious programming believed that she was going to die at 46 years of age and that there would be no point in moving forward or taking any action because she was going to die anyway.

Using Time Line Therapy®, we got to the root cause of this pain. Her unconscious mind took her back to the first significant event which triggered this behaviour which had been passed down through her bloodline, from three generations ago. The emotion *was fear of dying* and the belief was *I'm going to die.*

As we began the elimination process, the client could visualise a lady lying in a bed, surrounded by her children and my client could feel her fear of dying as she confirmed that both the emotion and the belief were true. By helping my client surrender her fears, change the script and reframe the limiting belief, she was able to effectively let the pain of the past and generational wounds go and replaced it with *"I can live my best life and be in the moment."*

When she came back, I asked her who she thought it could be and she had no idea. The next day she sent me a message and said she spoke to her sister about what she saw. Her sister replied that their great grandmother passed away at the same age, giving birth to a child. This was how the fear and the limiting belief had been passed down through each generation, onto her grandfather who died at 46, then onto her father, who also died at 46, and then passed onto my client who has now thankfully released it.

Can you see now how what you think the problem is, is never really the problem? It's always going to be something much deeper.

Honestly, I am always mind blown by the realisations the clients have.

She messaged me again yesterday and told me that she can't even make herself procrastinate anymore and it felt really strange!

When we experience something new and consciously we want to love it with all our heart, the inner voice creeps in and instead of embracing the new with deep empowerment, we react to how we have conditioned ourselves to be based on our experiences. The negative emotions attached to events in the past keep resurfacing causing you to react the way you do, even if you don't want to.

For example, when I first released the deep-rooted emotion of anger when I became a practitioner, my subconscious mind took me back to a memory of three past lives ago. I recalled a man with a top hat, screaming at a crying baby who was wrapped up tight like a mummy. Upon releasing this attachment and coming back in the now, Daniel asked me, *"Who was that in the memory?"*

Not realising that it was me, I suddenly felt my chest feel free. I had suffered with panic attacks and asthma for so long and it was as if in that moment, I had finally released the tightness in my chest. This emotion that caused my physical body so much pain had nothing to do with anything in this lifetime – it was in fact, a past life.

Someone once asked me, *"if I release this anger, does that mean I will stop being angry?"* Of course, it doesn't. It's an emotion. We will all feel emotions no matter what it is; it's just how we manage them to effectively create the life that we want. If there is a behaviour within you, that you don't understand why you do what you do and it causes you pain in the present, then this process will eliminate the root cause of the pain to reframe and reprogramme your subconscious mind. Instead of worrying about the future, you begin to trust it as you become more present by releasing the old way of thinking, feeling and behaving behind.

The only way you're ever going to clear the clutter and to truly start tapping into yourself, is when you give yourself permission and committing to change, to rewire your mind by releasing your trapped emotions and eliminate your limiting beliefs.

∞

I'M JUST NOT GOOD ENOUGH

100% of my clients have come to me with the belief that they *are not good enough*. In fact, around 90-95% of the population have this limiting belief which prevents most people from not trusting themselves because of the lack of belief within themselves.

My deep-rooted limiting belief that was really sabotaging me to move forward to be a success, a great mother, a wife, and a coach was also ***I'm not good enough***.

If you look back at my life, within the first ten years of my life, I had every type of abuse you could think of from sexual, physical, mental and emotional. My dad left when I was nine, leaving me feeling rejected and hurt.

The next decade, I self-harmed, seeked approval and I just wanted to fit in. I was desperately seeking love and attention and I really had no idea of who I was.

The following decade, I was completely intoxicated on drugs and in debt. I really struggled to settle in a relationship and I ended up with a few narcissistic men.

I thought perhaps it was all of *these* events that created the belief that I wasn't good enough. I mean, my teachers told me I was going to fail and that I would never get into sixth form; my friends never stuck around and I was constantly rejected by men; I was unable to land a permanent role in the city as I lacked financial security, and I was always arguing with my family.

It's just the way things are. I'm just not good enough.

Despite having this deep-rooted belief embedded in my mind, I still had this tenacity that kept me moving forward. Thankfully by working with Jo, we got to the root cause and eliminated this belief once and for all.

Using Time Line Therapy®, my subconscious mind took me back to when I was eight months in the womb. Now it hadn't been that long since I had passed my practitioner training and I was slightly dubious; but I trusted it and surrendered to the change because **I had enough** of feeling this way.

In the memory, I could see my mum sitting on a sofa, looking sad and down whilst she was pregnant with me. She was living with my grandparents at the time and I could feel the presence of my granddad in the vision. I could also see my dad pacing up and down in the room shouting at my mum, but I wasn't sure what he was saying, but I could feel how angry he was.

Thankfully Jo helped me shift my perception of this event to one of more joy, love and happiness as I began to believe more than ever **that I am good enough**! *When I left the memory, I swear I looked like a golden Buddha baby!*

> ***To shift from the old belief to the new is about transforming what you used to think and feel to how you want to think and feel by taking back your power and owning your goddamn self!***

Despite feeling amazing, I still had to check to see if any of this *was really true*. I called my mum and told her what I saw and with complete shock she replied:

"Yes, that's exactly what happened."

*"It was when we were living at granddad's old house. Your granddad was in the kitchen and I was sitting on the sofa, eight months pregnant with you, and I was looking out of the window because your dad was shouting at me. He was saying 'She's not my baby! Get rid of it!' and he was really angry. So I just sat there silently listening, because all I kept thinking was, **I'm not good enough** to be a mum, **I'm not good enough** to be a parent. **I'm just not good enough.**"*

And there it was. The limiting belief that kept me so stuck was NOT even mine - it was passed through to me via my mum. Looking back now it made *so much sense* as to why I felt so rejected in life and why I didn't feel worthy of existence, because my dad didn't even want me causing me to not even feel good enough for him. There I was, growing in the womb, absorbing everything my mum was thinking and feeling but also what my dad was saying and feeling too.

I also would like to add here that this was not my mum's fault. She had no idea that she would pass this belief onto me or even know what type of life that I would live. But that's how powerful the unconscious mind is, and no matter what you think or feel, you can always change the way you do. **Love you mum!**

95% of my clients release their limitations from either in the womb, during birth or past generations, which is why it's so important to surrender your past and forgive your loved ones by taking responsibility for how you're currently thinking, feeling and behaving because you cannot keep blaming your family. There were many family members who caused me a lot of pain and grief, including my own dad, but if I kept this anger and resentment inside, then I wouldn't be moving forward with my life. No one deserves abuse or trauma – NO ONE. But we also don't have to carry the pain either.

We never forget the past, but we can change the way we think, feel and behave about it by rewiring the subconscious. This is the power of the mind and WHY it's important - **so important** - that if you ever want to change the way you look at things, the things inside must change, as the limiting beliefs and negative emotions could potentially not even be yours!

∞

NO MEMORY IS EVER SILLY

Most people think they know what the problem is and why they feel the way they do, but I can 100% guarantee that you do not. I'm not here to impose anything but believe you me, your subconscious mind is so powerful, it's just impossible to understand the first root event of any experience that causes you pain unless you go through this process.

135

In 2019 a client reached out to me because she had just had enough. She was sobbing on the phone, massively in the victim mindset, and felt like everyone was out to make her life miserable. We worked together on a one-on-one basis, and literally within weeks, by applying her newfound self, she was able to change and transform her life, when she once thought it was never possible.

At the time she was barely making four figures a month but within weeks of her coaching it soon became multiple four figure weeks to five figure months as her business exploded! However, despite having this amount of success so quickly, something was stopping her from connecting with other empowering women. She had a fear of talking to people, but she couldn't establish what the root cause of this belief was.

Using Time line Therapy®, her subconscious mind recalled a memory of when she was five years of age at her dad's work dinner party. She saw herself approaching her dad's boss and saying to him, *"My dad doesn't like you. He thinks you are mean!"* Well! You can only imagine what her dad said to her after that.

*"You are **NEVER** allowed to speak to management again! You are **NEVER** coming to the events and because of your actions, your siblings are going to suffer too!"*

It was this significant event in her lifetime that caused her to feel extremely scared and sad with the belief that she couldn't *speak to management*. She had become fearful of approaching other empowering women because she was told that she couldn't.

This client was finally able to let this memory go with love and release the belief. She felt empowered, confident and so happy with herself that her entire energy shifted allowing her business to take off to another level as she reached multiple five figure months by being able to effectively communicate. This is how quick and powerful the mind-releasing process is and in fact, on average, it takes most of my clients around fifteen minutes per emotion and belief, pending on the pre-work that I have to do.

The past is the past, but it doesn't determine your future, which is why being in the now is so important. Before any change enters your life, no matter how big or small, we must first declutter - LITERALLY AND INTERNALLY and by doing so, you make room for internal peace and total happiness from within, with the confidence and deep knowingness that your life is heading in the right direction.

Pretty epic stuff, right?

NOW you should know how powerful the mind is and how it impacts your present.

NOW you know the true way of eliminating the blocks, negative emotions and limiting beliefs that are holding you back.

NOW you should know that no memory is ever silly and anything you are currently thinking and feeling that causes you to act in a way that you don't want to behave like, it can be changed into a way, that you do.

THIS IS THE POWER OF THE DEEP SUBCONSCIOUS WORK AND WHY I AM ONE OF THE UK'S LEADING MINDSET EXPERTS WHEN IT COMES TO RELEASING SELF-SABOTAGE.

On my website www.samevansglobal.com under success stories, you will find many more stories like this with client reviews, interviews and testimonials. Why not check them out, because if it's possible for them, then know, that it is possible for you too.

∞

Δ JOURNAL PROMPT Δ

Grab your journal, it's time to reflect!

Make a list with three columns:

- ***The first column (AGE)*** is for you to write down your age, starting with the earliest age that you can remember; ***the second column (EVENT)*** is to write down any negative events that you could have experienced from as young as you can remember; ***and the third column (BLOCK)*** is for stating any negative emotion that come up for you or limiting beliefs you believe to be true.
- *What patterns can you see that have been occurring, based on your life experiences?*
- *Looking at the third column, do you feel that any of these negative emotions and limiting beliefs could potentially NOT be yours?*
- *What would you like to believe and feel instead of the current negative emotions and limiting beliefs?*
- *How do you feel about forgiving your past now and how could it change your life?*

Place your hand on your heart, and say out loud;
"It's safe for me to surrender my past with ease. I am allowed to flow in the present with joy. I am ready to let it all go. It's safe for me to be."

Remember, if some of your beliefs are so deeply rooted and you need a block buster professional, reach out. You are never alone.

THE HEART

∞

Although I had deeply reprogrammed my subconscious mind, I still felt this pain in my heart that wouldn't shift. Speaking to a fellow coach, she pondered on whether I had healed properly.

It triggered me big time as I couldn't understand why she would say that because I was the mindset expert, wasn't I?

In 2020, I was so stressed out with my launching process and I was having an emotional breakdown simply because **I wasn't getting out of my own way.** I realised that this behaviour had to have stemmed from somewhere because after releasing so many negative emotions and limiting beliefs, you would have thought that I would have been 100% free. But at the time, I only specialised in the mind, not the heart and it was at this point I realised not only was I about to burst through another level, but

I was going to have another *fucking* breakthrough.

I started hearing more about the inner child and I wanted to learn more on what it was all about and how it was important to heal it as I already worked with clients by helping them release the negative attachments from their past.

Upon my discovery and having educated myself further, I discovered that the inner child is unconscious and something that is considered as a valid part of the human psyche. It's the part of us that represents the innocence, joy, wonder and playfulness, as well as sensitivity and other such qualities that we have, especially in the early years.

If you take a look back in the last chapter, most of our destructive patterns of behaviour and mental difficulties experienced are related to when we were a child as this causes our emotional, behavioural and relationship difficulties affecting our EQ.

We are told *to grow up, stop being sensitive, move on* and are taught to stifle and bury our emotions causing our inner child to feel rejected, neglected, and abandoned. We then carry these childhood fears, traumas and negative emotions into the present, causing us as adults to become disassociated with who we really are and become resistant to change.

No wonder we feel so misaligned!

My childhood had caused my mind to store many traumatic events from my past which I lovingly released; however, I had no idea how much my heart was really hurting.

As a child I was so tenacious and always **wanted and got my own way.** I wouldn't take any crap from anyone, *including my mum,* no matter how much trouble I used to get in and always knew how to defend myself, especially at home. I suffered tremendous amounts of physical abuse from my dad but despite the beatings leaving me shaken up and petrified, I would brush it off like it was nothing as if this deep strength from within me would keep me going as I learned to protect myself. This protective boundary created my defence mechanism which caused me to react instead of responding, as I slowly disconnected from my inner child.

You can see why now I couldn't love back and why I kept having these explosive outbursts.

Instead of making wise decisions as an adult with the best intentions, I couldn't self-direct myself because I was being guided by the wounded and rejected inner child as my heart was truly hurting, causing me to throw my dolls out of the pram, because I wasn't getting **my own way.** *Can you see how I grow through what I go through to help others?*

This is how I created the **Oneness Method**.

I discovered by using the power of hypnotherapy that you can speak to the inner child and understand what he/she is holding onto, to then go on to healing the deep wounds. By seeing this method as a separate entity from a client's point of view, this has helped them to disconnect from any of the harsh judgemental feelings they may have about themselves and instead, tap into the empathy and compassion that they would give to any suffering child as they reconnected to their inner child.

This method, *just like I did at the prime age of 41*, has allowed many of my clients to release the deep-rooted pains from the heart and has allowed them to transform their life within weeks and by doing so, they begin to feel empowered enough to re-parent themselves. This is why I tend to apply this method after the initial reprogramming of the subconscious mind.

Here are some examples of what clients have told me under deep hypnosis as I spoke to their inner child:

I don't feel acknowledged.
I can't express myself.

I am lonely.
I am lost.
I feel the need to protect myself because I'm going to get hurt.
I don't trust anyone.
I'm not safe.
I'm damaged.
I'm not special.
I'm not loved.

These deep-rooted beliefs and emotions had caused the clients major discomfort in their present life as they lacked the ability to trust themselves and communicate clearly. In helping them release their disconnected feelings and reconnect to their inner child, I have found that because their values change to what's important to them, it has allowed my clients to deeply reconnect to their infinite power at a whole new level. Without the need of being in control, they begin to embrace the fun and joy within their lives as they unlock their potential and manifest their desires, simply by healing their heart.

One particular client healed her inner child wounds, and told me:

"Sam, I feel complete. I feel so connected to my inner child. I just feel oneness with who I really am."

That was a proud moment for me because it showed me just how much this method is life changing as the ***once rejected child becomes embraced and accepted as their one true self.***

∞

△ JOURNAL PROMPT △

Grab your journal, darling; it's time to do some deep inner work.

- *What do you believe is the main cause of the disconnection from your inner child?*
- *What do you feel is the main cause of the disconnection from your inner child?*
- *How would connecting to your inner child transform your life?*
- *How would you like to think, feel and behave, if you reconnected to your inner child?*
- *What does connecting to your oneness look like and feel like?*
- *What will it allow you to achieve by connecting to the oneness that you are?*
- *How can you bring your oneness into the present now?*

Place your hand on your heart, and say out loud,

"It's safe for me to be me. It's safe for me to reconnect to my inner child. It's safe for me to have fun and to be me. It's safe to be me."

WELL DONE.

THE BODY

∞

So, is mindset really everything?

I used to think so. I used to think nothing in this world would ever work unless you worked on your mind which is true - **it's the first step to everything.**

As you become more present in the moment as the soulful self you truly are, the elimination of your subconscious limitations is vital to allow manifestation, achievement and alignment to truly flow into your life. It's what allows you to have trust and faith in all that you do as you become an expression of your soul's purpose.

But If 95% of your behaviours (your habits, the way you move, react and carry your physical body) are determined by your subconscious mind, then why is it that you don't feel in alignment with your new thought process?

You may be thinking, ***well hang on!*** *If I have just released my mental blocks, won't that release my physical blocks?* YES - it can; *especially illnesses.* But, if your physical body is determined by your subconscious programming, you will need to release the self-sabotage from your body too. This is why most people feel out of alignment.

It's as if *your mind is telling you YES! But your body…YOUR body's telling you…*

I'm going back to bed!

∞

Back in March 2021, I felt this incredible amount of stress on my body *doing the million courses I had signed up to*, as I pushed myself harder within my business.

In my head I felt amazing, but my body was not responding to most of my new found beliefs and I couldn't understand why which frustrated me even more. As much as I had released the trapped emotions and beliefs from my subconscious mind and I was instilling new ways of thinking and feeling, *my behaviour was not always in alignment.*

My habits were not always consistent with my thoughts.

I remember feeling this sweep of energy knock me down as if a hand was pushing me down, telling me, '***Please stop, rest, and think***.' What felt like a forever feeling of exhaustion, I just had enough and I knew another freaking breakthrough was about to happen.

I had this intense pain in my right shoulder which I do believe started in July 2019, but I just kept brushing it away until September 2020, when I was massively thrown into my work. I kept going to my osteopath and she couldn't even understand as to why it wouldn't go away however, what she did sense was that I was working too hard. Even my friends were telling me, *"Sam, you work so hard all the time! I don't know how you do it."*

And if I'm honest, NEITHER DID I.

Now, me being me, with my conditioning of *working hard,* I chose to keep going and ignore the pain. *"I can't be working too much. I haven't reached my targets! I've got a business to build! I haven't got time for all this!"*

We have been conditioned to believe that we need to *work hard,* do *the nine to five,* and work fifty-sixty hours a week to make money so that we can retire, get a pension, (which pays next to nothing), so then we can die. **That's not how life is supposed to be**. Life really is what we make it and it's only when we wake up and smell the coffee, that we can start to create significant changes in our lives.

I then started to notice that a lot of different coaches were talking about masculine and feminine energy. I felt my inner voice speak to me again, telling me that this pain was something to do with my masculine energy.

The masculine energy is referred to as the *doing* energy and is based on the right side of your body. It's the part of us that hustles, works hard, without a lot of emotional connection and it's about giving, which most of us have been conditioned to do. Whereas the feminine energy on the left side of your body, is referred to as *being in flow.* This side is all about trusting and having faith that everything will always work out.

Some people say, *"You got to be more feminine!"* Some people say, *"You got to be more masculine!"* Some people say, *"Fuck it! don't do anything - JUST MOVE!"* **But do you know what I say?** *Just do what feels right for you.* It's about really listening to yourself because when you do, you just know what feels right for you, **your way**.

Heal the mind, heal the heart, heal the body.

It was at this point I was introduced to the world of silent counselling. This modality diffuses the negative emotions that cause severe stress to the body. By connecting to the meridians in the face, the body and in the hands, you can effectively release any self-sabotage from the body's energy system with the power of breathing.

When I had my own silent counselling session, I couldn't believe how much this pain in my shoulder was causing a major impact in my ability to just be. I didn't know how to be chilled out because all I ever knew was how to hustle. My entire life I have worked hard, with two to three jobs and I didn't know how to be any other way. But when we work for ourselves, it's supposed to be fun, not boring, because you ain't working for someone else, you are working for yourself!

When I released the blockages from my body, it not only allowed me to listen to myself more, but it also allowed the shoulder pain to disappear and allowed me to release two more limiting beliefs that were also holding me back.

"*I have to make enough money to pay for bills*" and "*I have to work hard for money.*" These deep-rooted limited beliefs were embedded from one to three generations ago and were causing me MUCH grief when it came to running my business with ease.

Not only did I release the fear and doubts from my mind, but by releasing the physical blockages from my body, I was able to trust and be in flow like this shift I have never felt before! I felt lighter, happier and more peaceful, just like my client earlier, who no longer needed to have her surgery.

You can do the work and be the person whilst having fun.

Work isn't supposed to be hard and money isn't just for paying the bills. It's a partner, someone who has your back whenever you need it and it's only by being in flow that you take the pressure off being yourself and become the person you really ought to be.

You can begin to stop forcing yourself to do the things you don't want to do.

You begin to realise when you are about to burn out and avoid it at all costs.

You realise your limits, allowing yourself to flow with ease, moment to moment, rather than day by day.

You trust yourself at a deeper and cellular level because YOU can now finally listen to YOUR GODDAMN SELF.

YOU FINALLY connect to your spirit.

∞

FIND YOUR FLOW

When you resist change, feel confused, or second guess, instead of allowing yourself to trust yourself, you push yourself harder, which in turn, causes you to feel a lot worse than you did before. In fact, it causes unease in the body because energetically, you are unable to flow with ease.

In this section I am going to share with you a simple technique to help you get into flow every single day. This process is called a polarity test.

This is such an effective tool if you are experiencing any negative attitudes and self-sabotaging behaviours that prevent you from connecting to your inner voice. When you feel like you can't, this is known as Psychological Reversal (PR), which actually blocks any kind of healing to the human body.

148

You could possibly be feeling irritable, woken up in a bad mood, your negative self-talk could have spiraled out of control, or you could be procrastinating.

If this is the case, to allow yourself to move from **PR** to a positive state, I would like to help you get into the flow by applying the following into your life which will allow your physical body to respond in a much calmer way to allow you to have that instant shift.

Step 1:

Using your two right fingers, rub the soft spot on the left side of the chest, just under the armpit while focusing on the issue that is causing you to feel negative. Whilst rubbing gently, inhale deeply and then exhale two breaths – the first a quick short burst with the second one slowly and longer. Repeat this three times.

Step 2:

Once you feel slightly calmer, use the two same right fingers and gently place them under your nose. This is the meridian point for personal trust and reassurance of internal change. Whilst gently rubbing, inhale deeply, and exhale two breaths – the first a quick short burst with the second one slowly and longer. Repeat this three times.

Step 3:

Finally, using the two right fingers again, tap the outside of your left hand on the side of the little finger, reconfirming the following positive affirmations – *"I am well, I am content, and I am in control. I am confident and I am safe, as me."* This is another meridian point for change so repeat this as many times as you desire.

I offer silent counselling sessions and I am now a trainer in this modality, so why not check out my website for more details or email me at <u>sam@samevansglobal.com</u> to either book in for your own session or to add it to your own coaching practice.

You can also use this method after each of the chapters once you have completed the tasks as you affirm the affirmations I have stated. Consciously remember that you are an incredible being and it's safe for you to be yourself.

YOUR SPIRIT

∞

Your spirit is everything; it's the inner voice, the gut feeling, the reason why sometimes when you meet someone you instantly take a dislike to them - that's your spirit. Over time, we become disconnected from it because we allow our humanness, our physical bodies to take control, controlled by our subconscious conditioning instilled from the moment we were conceived.

I had to go through some dark times to connect and embrace my own spirit which meant I had to let go of my need to seek external sources of validation to know whether I was worthy or not. I had seriously lost myself by giving away my power which was causing me major internal conflicts as I completely lacked in my ability to trust myself.

∞

In 1978 my mum told my dad that she was pregnant. He was not impressed and told her, *"Get rid of it."* My mum did what she was told and as she was only a few weeks pregnant, she booked an appointment within days because all she wanted to do was to keep my dad happy.

On the day of the abortion, she was told by the doctors that if she went ahead with it, she would never be able to have children again because she was twelve weeks pregnant, not five. Now my mum, never having been with another man before my dad, freaked out and called my granddad who advised her to come straight home. My dad then went onto a spiral of abuse at my mum accusing her of cheating.

That night, both my nanny and my mum had a vision, a dream, that a child would be born on the 25th of July and that she would be special. And oh yes! That would be me!

This is why I believe deep in my soul why my purpose has always been bigger than me as this was my divine plan as mentioned in the introduction, about the time when I was seven years old.

∞

I'm not woo-woo, or religious; I'm super-spiritual, intuitive and guided.

God was drummed into me from a very young age and I honestly don't know where I would be if my family hadn't of taught me about God. I know he exists. I know he's out there and I know he hears my prayers. This is not for me to impose my beliefs onto you; just for you to understand me and how I got to where I am now.

I'm never going to tell you what you should or shouldn't do - you have to do what feels right for you. However, when I tapped into my spirit, so much in my life changed. YES, I do a lot of inner work and empowering training on myself because anything I ever need to work on, the answer is within me; but it wasn't until I connected to my infinite power, by healing my connection with the Divine, that I was finally able to break free and listen.

I believe that religion has caused a lot of chaos in the world creating beliefs that potentially cause us to judge and feel disconnected from others whereas culture, I believe creates more of how we should respond and how we should behave, preventing us from being our true selves.

As much as I understood my religion, my culture was completely different. I was born into a Sikh family and the religion itself is one of peace whereas my culture was very strict and disciplined where I was unable to do many things like the other girls in East London, such as wear short clothes, drink alcohol and party til early hours of the morning, which as an Indian girl, it was so frowned upon. The one thing I have to say about my culture and upbringing is that respect was huge and for that, I am forever grateful.

Despite having so much faith in God, there was also a lot of superstition that my family had nurtured my mind to also believe. Such as, *don't laugh too much, you will cry. Don't look too pretty, you will get too many compliments and you will get bad luck. Don't do this and don't do that!* No wonder I was such a wild child and adamant to do things my way, because as a manifestor I did not like to be controlled.

In 2019, as I began to deeply focus on my mindset coaching, I was offering complimentary calls to women before they enrolled into my one-on-one coaching. One particular lady was ever so depressed that she loved the idea of how Time Line Therapy® could completely help her let everything go. Now I had only just completed a four-month intensive with Jo, so I was super fresh and excited to help people. But this particular lady told me something that completely freaked me out.

"Sam, I am so excited to do this and I am so glad you told me about this method. I see things moving around all the time and I believe I was burned at the stake because I was a witch in a past life."

Well did I freak the fuck out when she told me this and was instantly triggered with tears, doubts and left feeling so, so scared!

I instantly messaged Jo, neurotic and crying, leaving a hundred messages as I told her **this has to go!** She jumped on a call with me to understand what this was about and to release the fear from my mind.

Thankfully she did and within minutes I felt free. She then went on to ask me if there were any other events that were linked to this emotion that I needed to release and if there were, if I knew how old I was. I screamed:

"OMG YES! WHEN I WAS 15!"

∞

THERE IS NO SUCH THING AS GOOD MAGIC

In the summer of 2014 we as a family, my grandparents, my mum and my two sisters, went to India for a six-week holiday. I hadn't been for almost 10 years and inside I was so sad because I didn't want to go. It was a nine-hour flight, then a nine-hour drive to the village and it absolutely stinks when you arrive. *(I wonder if this is why I have a low threshold for bull shit?!)*

By the time we arrived in our gorgeous village, I was exhausted yet excited to be there. Punjab is such a beautiful place, and it felt so peaceful to finally be home. I walked into my granddads house and there was this lady there who was just about to leave. As she left, my mum frantically went on to tell me and my two sisters that she was a witch and she does a lot of black magic and to make sure that if we ever combed our hair, to burn any that fell out, **otherwise she would make a voodoo doll.**

FFS!

Not something I really wanted to hear, but I accepted it and went to sleep. In the middle of the night between midnight and 3am, I felt something over me and I woke up screaming!

"Someone's done something to me! I can feel it! They've put blood on me!"

My nanny came rushing in and instantly did something to calm me down. My family has a lot of methods that can bring peace into your soul and this was when I really began to give my power to outside sources to bring me inner peace. Again, I love my nanny to bits and it wasn't her fault, she only wanted to protect me and that is all that matters because that night,

my spirit had been attacked in my sleep by some crazy witch.

Once I released my attachment to this event, I came back and realised everything made sense.

Before the age of fifteen, despite the beatings, the sexual abuse and emotional trauma, I was pretty strong and tough in myself. But when I returned from this holiday, between the ages of 15 to 35 years of age, my emotional and erratic behaviour spiralled out of control. You can call it coincidence, you call it whatever you want, but in that moment of releasing, I realised that it was when I was fifteen that I had in fact started to project my chaos into my outer world and the main reason why I acted the way that I did because my spirit had been attacked.

I started buying stones, crystals, reading star signs and obsessed with tarot card readings because I just wanted to know that all was going to be ok as I couldn't trust myself and I would have done anything to just feel calm and peaceful.

It wasn't until I awoke to my truth, when I tapped into the divine in 2019 as I started to read scriptures from the bible. Again, I am not religious, but I know there is a higher purpose than me and I had to seriously heal my spirit. My inner voice was telling me that the only way to do this was to improve my faith in God.

I had no idea that spirit was and is everything and how much I was blocking my ability to tap into it. I always did feel however, that every time I cried for no reason, this was my spirit trying to talk to me; but my protective ego didn't want me to get hurt again because of how disconnected I was from my inner child. My physical body held onto so much pain and trauma that I projected it everywhere I went, which caused me to react instead of respond. I never knew that my past, my conditioning and my programming from the outside world would prevent me from being my true self.

I remember one time I had this weird dream about this ring I used to wear with an orange stone. I was told at seventeen that I had to wear it all the time and I should never take it off or it will impact my sexuality. **What a fucking dick I was**. In 2019 I had this intuitive feeling to ask my husband what I should do with it and he said, "***get rid of it***" and so I did. Safe to say, the ring did nothing for me and I am with the man of my dreams so, all is good!

It's taken me a good ten years to do this research, to experience this journey to become the best version of myself and I wouldn't be here if my hubby hadn't of guided me, who I do believe was sent to me from God. He is my living guide and I do believe spirit talks through him to help me. *Like the time I asked him for the truth earlier on about friendships and about the ring.*

I was no longer controlled by other things to help me remain calm and cool – **I listened to me.**

I was no longer conditioned by my past – **I became me.**

I was no longer living in fear or worrying about the future – **I believe in me.**

By surrendering my past, healing my heart, releasing my physical pain and connecting to spirit, I became energetically aligned - mentally, emotionally, physically, financially, and spiritually. This is how I feel every day.

This is the infinite power of alignment empowered as one.

This is the power of healing, and this is why the inner work is never done, unless you keep being you!

∞

PART IV
INTEGRATION

You were born to be more than just mediocre.

When you have bat shit crazy faith, your prayers are always heard.

The answers could come up in a random post on social media, or from a stranger, or from a quote, or from a family member.

Always know that you are guided, so listen to your inner voice and if you ever feel you made a poor decision, it's OK. Mistakes happen.

Learn your lesson, let it go.

Your energy is far too precious.

AUTHENTICALLY ALIGNED

∞

I hope you now understand how vital it is to reprogram your mind, heart and body and how becoming aligned to your most empowered self is literally feeling happy and joyful with the decisions you make without resistance, without second-guessing yourself, without having to question from a place of confusion, as you tap into the infinite being that you are.

To be in an energetic alignment with balance, flow and the utmost belief in what you want and where you need to go, is when you are deeply connected to spirit by aligning yourself mentally, physically and emotionally. You have trust, faith and clarity in all that you do and all that you are, by flowing in balance with your masculine and feminine energy and surrendering your needs and wants as you become your soulful self.

It kind of feels like everything falls into place, where you are no longer burning out, or feeling exhausted, as if there is a deeper connection to your identity, which in turn allows you to constantly be in the flow of success without feeling the need of rushing, speeding or racing.

The Cognitive Switch® has transformed my life and so many of the women's lives I have worked with and now, you have the gift to be able to apply the tools into your life too, so you can become an empowered freaking badass without the self-sabotage!

I really hope that you have felt some major breakthroughs or had some phenomenal lightbulb moment as to why things haven't shifted in your life and you now know what you need to do. I asked my good friend Claire to read this book before it was printed, and she told me that she unlocked a deep-rooted belief simply by reading it! That to me shows just how powerful this book can and will be if you apply the tools into your life.

We, as women, can really have it all, know it all and reach our potential, when we deeply believe that **WE CAN**, in complete alignment.

The power is within you. When you tap into it, you won't ever doubt yourself again.

BECAUSE YOU REALLY ARE WORTH IT.

MUTHA EFFIN' MONEY BLOCKS!

∞

In 2019, a coach was sending me all these things to help me with my money mindset because I had no problem making it, I just couldn't get it fast enough!

"SAM! YOU HAVE GOT TO REMOVE YOUR MONEY BLOCK, GIRL!"

And I literally thought to myself,

IF I FUCKING KNEW WHAT IT WAS, I WOULD GET RID OF IT!

When I became a parent, I was so obsessed with making money. I just wanted to replace the weekly four figure income I used to get as an Executive Assistant in the city and I knew that the only way to achieve this was by running my own business.

I literally would cry so hard watching everyone make shit loads of money, buy the books, do the rituals, but still NADA! I kid you not, I bought every mindset book going. I was told to be joyous, be present, be in the moment, everything will come, but it didn't because deep down, I FELT LIKE CRAP.

I was massively in my own way when it came to allowing money to flow to me with ease and one of the reasons why I invested so much time, money and energy into coaching was because there had to be a way to overcome this block. Here I was, helping my clients earn five figure months, and launching businesses from scratch, manifesting their dream homes *but why was it not working for me?*

> *You can't say I'm BROKE every single day and then decide to say I AM A MILLIONAIRE!*

Of course, it's possible, but your body thinks you're lying because of your memories in the mind. It's too much for your brain to comprehend. if you have habits of worrying and acting in a particular way around money, your money story was formed before you most probably even knew that it was created, exactly like your subconscious programming of yourself.

One of my gorgeous mentors, Lisa Johnson, told me that I should really talk about money mindset. At first, I couldn't see how, but the more I investigated it, I realised that I have been helping women with their money mindsets from the moment I began coaching.

I remember one day, I was sitting on the sofa watching TV, completely NOT thinking of work or money, and my hubby mentioned something to me about how I used to be in 2013.

I had just found out that I was pregnant with my second in 2012, and we were living in a one-bedroom flat. I decided to move out with a one-year-old into a two-bedroom flat without any concern for my hubby. Pretty selfish behaviour, but I was so wrapped up in myself, I couldn't trust that everything would work out, even though he told me to have faith.

I was working part-time in the nursery and I wasn't even struggling with money, even though I felt as if I was. But I made a decision without consideration of my husband, I felt massively alone and thought that money was going to run out. My family were supporting me by sending me a lot of money and I was always rescued; but my lack of belief that I could make so much money myself, was causing me major grief, harming my relationship with money and with my loved ones.

There was something in his words from this message that began to trigger off all these memories in the mind with my behaviour, my actions, and the results that I achieved when it came to money and right there and then, I had this lightbulb moment as I had just discovered my money block!

"I cannot be trusted with money; I have to always borrow!"

It all made sense because my entire life, I had always been rescued with money as I lacked the belief that I could make it myself! At 7, I stole money from my mum's purse; At 15, I got a mobile phone under my mum's name and she always paid my bills; At 18, I was very mischievous with money. I would take out store cards, which again my mum was always paying off for me. At 19, I got my first credit card and by the time I was 21, I had accrued over 40k in debt. At 23, I was in an IVA; At 30, I was bankrupt; At 32, I went from earning £3.5k a month to the government maternity pay. I had to borrow to live – earn, borrow, spend, borrow, borrow, borrow, borrow!

I cried as soon as I realised this because never in my life, did I ever think my behaviour was anything to do with my money block. But of course, it was! A money block is just a limiting belief and because I was always rushing, panicking and worrying about not having enough money I allowed money to be the problem, instead of allowing it to be my friend because of my past money story. It was so deeply embedded, and I knew I just had another major breakthrough.

Can you see WHY turning a positive into a negative won't cut it because you already have the habit integrated into the mind-body connection because of your past?

Your money blueprint has most probably been instilled through generations of beliefs and behaviours, causing you to respond based on what you know already, because of your upbringing.

For me, my belief stemmed from when I was in the womb. By releasing it, I have an amazing relationship with money because I no longer allow it to consume me with stress, fears, or worries. I finally took back my power which allowed me to breathe, to trust, and always have faith that income will always flow whenever I need it, at the right time. I began to change the way I managed my income and stopped borrowing and getting myself into debt with credit cards and loans.

By applying the method with the women I was working with, I realised another baby was born.

Introducing **Unlock Your Money Block®** my money mindset transformational programme that has helped so many women unleash their earning potential by completely transforming their money mindset with a belief system like never before.

This technique works deeper in the unconscious mind because I guarantee, you have no idea how much power you have given money nor know where the block even began. You deserve to know why you feel blocked and how you can achieve so much more!

Now, I'm not saying that you will manifest a million pounds overnight. But instead of having the old beliefs **consumed with mutha-effin money blocks,** you start to think what's possible, you start to take back your power with money, you start to behave differently, you act and feel differently because your money relationship has been healed.

The relationship between you and money is no different to that of with another person. If you talk about money in a negative way, you will keep getting more negativity. So again, mind your tongue!

Money flows to you when you show up and take action. *Not by rubbing fairy dust all over your workspace and waiting for it to fall into yourlap!* Making money is supposed to be easy and we aren't supposed to work hard, graft like a dog or hustle every day.

You can flick that money switch from scarcity to abundance, just like me and all the other women I have served, when you Unlock your Money Block® and place a new belief in the mind. Everything begins within you.

Δ **READY TO LEARN MORE?**Δ

I run this particular programme at least twice a year. Feel free to message me at sam@samevanslgobal.com to enrol or if you want to ask me more about this programme.

INTENSIFY YOUR INTENTIONS®

∞

Ah! I am so excited that you have reached this part of the book. As much as I have all the tools, knowledge, wisdom and crazy stories to back up what I do, the power now lies within you to achieve your desires.

As much as the inner work and the subconscious reprogramming is powerful, and required in each and every one of us, the results that we achieve will come from our actions that we take, whilst being the person we desire to be.

By having bat shit crazy faith, you overcome any fears, doubts and overwhelm as you know exactly what you need to do, when you need to do it.

So what next? What will you do now to make your desires happen?

You gotta Intensify Your Intentions®!

If intention is how you desire to be, and achieving your goals is where you want to be, the power is always going to come from who you are NOW, in this moment.

I know what it's like when you get so excited for something - an intention to be, to have whatever it is you want; the difficulty in letting go of the outcome and trusting in the moment; You try so hard to not think about it, focus on it or let it consume your world as you try to control your thoughts and feelings; but instead you end up having an argument with yourself:

"Perhaps it won't happen, but what if it does! OMG, WHAT IF IT DOES? Yeah, but I don't want to get my hopes up? Yeah, but you can't think negatively, or you will attract it? Ok. So, I won't get it."

I know people say that goals are important as it helps you to achieve them faster if you write down the exact date of when you want them; YES. It's true in some respect, but the one thing I feel helps to have them arrive faster is if you let go of time and have trust in the outcome.

The obsession with time and outcome causes a disconnection from being in flow with the belief that it's possible. It's ok to want things; it's ok to work towards things; it's ok to have a plan; it's ok to have a strategy; *but wouldn't it be better to just be with ease instead of pressure?*

Going with the flow doesn't mean you don't have any business plans in place - NOT AT ALL! It means having a plan of action, a desire with an intention to be, whilst enjoying every single moment in the present.

Back in 2018 I started a goals jar. I wrote down my goals and desires of what I wanted to achieve and around 25% of them, I dated. I put the exact time and date of when I wanted to achieve them. The others I just left as deep-rooted desires with the belief and intention that it is possible.

A year later, I opened the jar and I noticed something peculiar.

The ones without dates, I achieved. The ones with, I did not. *I actually opened this jar live on Facebook sharing exactly what I HAD achieved. I think I actually cried because I couldn't believe what I had achieved.*

As soon as I finished the live show, I decided to set my goals and desires for the following year. I went through all the ones I had achieved, and the ones I didn't and as I read the ones with the dates, I was sent another message from spirit.

"Well if you don't trust me, why should I give it to you?"

And that's when it hit me hard! I always had this feeling that setting exact dates just puts pressure on you because it really hinders your inability to let go of the outcome. *But why date them?* If I received the other ones within that time frame without a date, then why did I put so much pressure on myself to achieve the ones with a date?

Having trust in your desires requires you to set those goals and surrender them. LET THEM GO! It's about becoming the person to achieve your goals NOW so when you do achieve them, it's as if it already happened.

For example, *remember my story about the bug infestation?* My obsession at the time was to move into a house from a flat, so I spent 2016, searching for a house in a particular part of London, but nothing felt right. I put my intention out there that I wanted a nice house, away from where we lived, with room and space, and a garden.

A year later, in the summer of 2017, my husband told me he had enough of the flat and he wanted to move. At this point, I was super happy, organised and content with the property and didn't actually want to move, *especially as I had become obsessed with cleaning!*

I called the letting agency in August and I asked if I could wait until September to move. They recommended that I just start looking now, as you never know.

Now, my hubby is six foot three and my children were growing fast, so I had to make sure there was enough space for us all, but they kept sending us to cottages. I had already stated clearly that I needed a big house, but it was either too small or out of our price range.

Two weeks later, I was on route to viewing the properties and again, they were all cottages, except for one. No link, no picture, just an address. So, me being me, curiosity got the better of me, and I googled the property. I was like *ok, looks like a nice area* and off I set to view the house.

As I was driving, I felt goosebumps all over my body, as the route that I was taking was towards the area I set my intentions to, a year earlier. I instantly began to cry, and said out loud, *"**OMG, YOU HEARD ME!**"* I felt as if my desires were here!

As soon as I arrived up at the property, I instantly fell in love and I was like, **THIS IS IT**. And it was. We are still here living in this gorgeous house. Now, my dream home is a five-bed detached house that we own. This is a three-bed semi-detached. *Am I going to be ungrateful?* Of course not. It's just a clear sign that I am on my way to my dream house and this is just all part of the journey. The reason why I received this house when I did was because I had become appreciative, considerate and lived in gratitude with what I had, instead of consumed with what I didn't have.

This is the power of intentions and when you ask and believe, you will receive and how I birthed my next baby, Intensify your Intentions®.

∞

171

Δ **READY TO LEARN MORE?**Δ

I run this programme Every December and my doors are always open. Feel free to message me at <u>sam@samevanslgobal.com</u> to enrol or if you want to ask me more about this programme.

THE FINALE

∞

You can and *will understand who you truly are and what you are capable of because you are deeply and utterly filled with such limitless potential and it wants to come out.*

You can let go of people's opinions and judgement, because you will tap into you, listen to your voice and understand what you do what and what you *don't, because you trust you.*

You can *tap into you and understand how you are, how you work, and make those internal connections, to what is possible for you.*

You can change the way you look at things as things you look at change *because you started looking into you.*
You have to power to have, be and do whatever you want, because I believe in you.

MY DEEPEST GRATITUDE TO YOU

∞

Becoming a Coach and Mentor was one of the best things I could have ever done in my life (after having my family of course)!

Knowing that the clients are achieving, knowing that they are progressing, that they are breaking free, they are taking charge and knowing that they don't need to rely on anyone else for solutions but to trust their intuition, by using their most valuable tool they have - their inner voice - IS THE MOST INCREDIBLE FEELING IN THE WORLD!

Success of others really does make me so HAPPY!
I always say, I am like your sofa! Lean on me, use me for support, but soon you will need to let go, and step up! Just like a baby learning to walk.

You have the right to be free and just be you!
You have the right to walk on your own two feet and know how to get back up when you stumble and fall.
It's just a matter of having someone to guide you with the right tools.

If you feel that you deserve more but don't know what it is or how to get there, if you feel that you are stuck somewhere or hitting a brick wall and have no idea how to break it down, if you are setting your goals too low, and not earning the potential you deserve and desire, then it's high time you start getting crystal clear on what it is you specifically want, and who you need to be to reach your goal.

Lives are changing and you deserve to be outside of the box - creating the life you desire, breaking free and just being your most authentic self, living your life to the max - instead of stuck in a box.

After all, how can you think outside the box, IF YOU ARE IN IT?

Embrace the change. Learn your lesson. Release the bull!

Make those changes today because you deserve success and it would be my absolute honour to help you achieve financial freedom and an unbreakable mindset.

From the bottom of my heart, I'm so grateful for you, for purchasing this investment for your growth and expansion. I would love to hear from you, so I have listed my social media links and website for you, as I really do look forward to connecting with you and hearing how you turned off self-sabotage and turned on self-empowerment, like a flick of a switch!

Much love to you.

Love always, Sam x

LET'S CONNECT

∞

There are many courses and programmes that I offer, and I would love to help you unleash your badass into the world, when you flick that cognitive switch! You can either go to my website or email me at sam@samevansglobal.com for more information. I also have many free gifts that are also available for you on my website.

check out my website for testimonials, freebies and courses at www.samevansglobal.com

you can email me at sam@samevansglobal.com

You can also follow me on the following social media sites, I can't wait to meet you!

facebook.com/samevansglobal1

instagram.com/samevans.coach

ABOUT THE AUTHOR

∞

Sam Evans, based in the UK, lives with her husband and two children and has, through her own self-development, created an empowering coaching practice that has globally helped heal the minds of hundreds of women in the online realm at a subconscious level.

As an accredited Master Coach in NLP, Timeline Therapy™, and Hypnotherapy, alongside her trademarked methods, The Cognitive Switch® and Unlock Your Money Block®, she has helped them confidently increase revenues of up to £1m, create thriving businesses, attract followers, and defeat self-sabotage, by guiding women to become decisive in action and clear in message, by overcoming their worst enemy: themselves.

Sam is an CREA 2021 Brainz award honouree, and has been featured on Fox, NBC and Mum Boss UK, Female First and Mental Magazine. Sam has also appeared on podcasts such as Coach Magazine, Andrew Kaplan's Shatter the Mold, and Hannah Marie Olivia's Adulting Advice; Guest speaker at the MIBA International, Women helping women grow summit, at the HerStory Global Summit.

Utilising her excellence as a UK approved TTi® Emotional Quotient Practitioner, specialising in Emotional Intelligence, Human Design, Inner Child Therapy and Silent Counselling, Sam's mission is to transform the lives of one million women, by diminishing the inner critic to access their infinite intelligence and potentiality by 2030.

She is also a number 1 best-selling Amazon author of Monetise Your Message and now the author of The Cognitive Switch®.

ACKNOWLEDGEMENTS

∞

As much as the work I put in helps so many people across the globe, I wouldn't be here if it wasn't for certain mentors, coaches and loved ones who saw my potential, before I could.

Firstly, I have to acknowledge My gorgeous husband, Barry. My god, where do I begin. You were the only man on this planet who saw my potential and who knew I was worth more, could be more, and do more. You saw me for who I could be, rather than who I was and if you hadn't of pushed me, I don't think I would be here. You helped me overcome the deepest pain I never thought I would ever overcome and you really showed me what true love is. I'm so grateful to you baby, because believe it or not, I DO LISTEN TO YOU, even when you think I don't!

Joshua and Micah. Two little dudes who seriously rock my world with joy. You bring me so much light in this life, and I dedicate this book to you, because I want you to know that if I can, believe you me, so can you. I love you boys.

My family - my mum, for giving birth to me, my grandparents for always being there, my sisters and everyone else; including my in-laws! I love you. I know when things were rough, I was an emotional wreck, but you were always there. You supported me, you guided me and never gave up on me and for that I am forever grateful.

Divena my bestie! You were the only friend I ever met who met me at rock bottom and stuck by me to where I am now. I freaking love you girl!

Claire. For reviewing my book last minute and checking my spelling errors! I'm so grateful to you.

Daniel Tolson. THANK YOU! Thank you for helping me see my potential and calling me on my own bullshit excuses. If you never saw through me, I don't think I would be an NLP Coach today. You helped me master my own emotional intelligence, taught me everything I know, which has helped me to guide so many women to become coaches themselves. Thank you for being you.

Jo Eva. Oh Jo! Where would I be without you! The random freaked out messages I used to send you when I was completely consumed with self-sabotage! Working with you changed my entire life and they were the best 18 months of my life. Thank you so much for helping me clear my own blockages and for allowing me to be a phenomenal coach.

Ewan Mochrie. Thank you. Thank you for helping me unlock the deepest potential that existed within me and helping me overcome my sexual abuse. The deepest block I had was causing me major panic and fear and without your mentoring, I wouldn't have overcome it. Thank you for helping me become a master coach.

My clients. I wouldn't be here if it wasn't for the women who trusted me, who reached out to me, and allowed me to be their guide. I'm so thankful to every single woman I have worked with because this journey couldn't have happened if you hadn't been in my life. YOU KNOW WHO YOU ARE!

Authors and Co. For this book would not have been possible, if you had not have given me the opportunity to put my knowledge, wisdom and wisecracks together to help reach the world with my powerful message. Thank you for your patience, guidance and support, I don't know what I would have done without you.

And most importantly, my heavenly father. If God wasn't in my life, I would never have unlocked my potential, none of these people would have been sent to me and I most certainly wouldn't be who I am today. I thank God every day for all that I have and I always will, especially for all that is to come.

I love you.

Thank you. Sam

Printed in Great Britain
by Amazon